Trading With China

Trading With China

How to Export Goods, Services & Technology to the Chinese Market

Danai Krokou

BEP

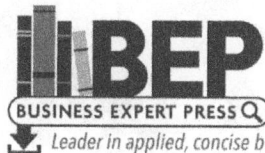

BUSINESS EXPERT PRESS

Leader in applied, concise business books

Trading With China:
How to Export Goods, Services & Technology to the Chinese Market

Cover design by Charlene Kronstedt

Interior design by Exeter Premedia Services Private Ltd., Chennai, India

First published in 2021 by
Business Expert Press, LLC
222 East 46th Street, New York, NY 10017
www.businessexpertpress.com

ISBN-13: 978-1-63742-127-7 (paperback)
ISBN-13: 978-1-63742-128-4 (e-book)

Business Expert Press International Business Collection

Collection ISSN: 1948-2752 (print)
Collection ISSN: 1948-2760 (electronic)

First edition: 2021

10 9 8 7 6 5 4 3 2 1

Description

China's rise to prosperity in recent decades coincided with the surge in global trade and falling protectionism. But as we are entering the third decade of the 21st century, the economic structure that prevailed in the West during the previous decades is now beginning to look very different. Global economic relationships are being redefined in the wake of the global financial crises, the recent U.S.–China trade tensions, Brexit, and the Covid-19 pandemic. However, when global trade suffers, so do local economies. In today's economy, international cooperation and open trade are not an option, but a necessity.

Trading With China is a concise and useful handbook to Western businesses, entrepreneurs, and investors doing business with or in China. It is also a practical guide of use to anyone considering to export goods, services, and technology to the Chinese market.

The book contains industry information, updated data, key models, practical advice, and strategy options for different types of companies and industry sectors. It details all relevant procedures, opportunities, and challenges by industry sector and geographical region. It discusses major issues such as market barriers, import requirements, distribution channels, labeling, and operational challenges. Topics covered in *Trading With China* also include relevant rules, regulations, documentation, and management issues related to the export of different types of goods, services, and technology to China.

Keywords

U.S.–China trade; global trade; U.S. export; U.K. export; post-Brexit trade; China import; international business development; foreign investment; Chinese market; technology export; services export; F&B export

Contents

Introduction

Trade has been a very significant factor of China's economy. In the 25 years that followed the founding of the Republic in 1949, China's trade institutions developed into a partially modern but somewhat inefficient system. The drive to modernize the economy began in 1978 and required a sharp acceleration in commodity flows, which resulted in improved efficiency in economic transactions. In the ensuing years, economic reforms were adopted by the government to develop a socialist market economy. This type of economy combined central planning with market mechanisms. These changes resulted in the decentralization and expansion of domestic and foreign trade institutions, as well as a greatly enlarged role for free markets in the distribution of goods and a prominent role for foreign trade and investment in economic development.

In 2019, global trade accounted for almost 60 percent of the global GDP, nearly up 1.5 times since 1980. Over the past four decades, international trade has transformed significantly, not only in terms of volume and composition but most importantly in terms of the countries that the rest of the world leans on for their most important trade and political alliances. Now a critical shift is about to occur and it may surprise you to learn that China has already usurped the United States as the world's leading trading partner.

The United States and China are competitors in many ways, but to be successful they must rely on each other for mutually beneficial trade. At the same time, global trade is the major issue on which they are struggling to reach a common ground. Also, China is a huge market for U.K. businesses in everything from technology to luxury products. The United Kingdom exported over £23 billion of goods and services to China in 2019, while the EU exported goods worth €198 billion the same year. China's gross domestic product (GDP) grew by around 10 percent a year, from the beginning of the market reforms in 1978 to the 2008 financial crisis. The headline figure has currently fallen to just over 7 percent as the Chinese government rebalances the economy to make growth more reliant on domestic consumption and less on investment.

The Chinese market often seems chaotic to most Western business people. This is partly true. In China, trading of goods is also trading of relationships. With rapid and continuous industrialization and urbanization, a vast and fast-growing consumer market has emerged. Bicycles and Mao suits have been substituted by 110 million cars. China is now the largest car market in the world, enjoying international labels and luxury goods. China is also the world's largest ICT market, with over 1.2 billion mobile subscribers as of 2018, and 564 million Internet users, that is, over 42 percent of its total population.

Key Growth Drivers and Trends

A major growth driver is the rapid increase in average household incomes. In fact, China's urban household income per capita increased from CNY 1,516 in 1990 to CNY 42,359.2 in 2019. As expected, high income earners spend a higher proportion of their revenues on higher value products and imported food, including milk products, prepackaged food, dining out, etc. The trend in the annual per capita food purchases shows a significant increase in dairy consumption and a decline in grain consumption.

Annual per capita disposable income of urban households in China from 1990 to 2019 in Chinese Renminbi

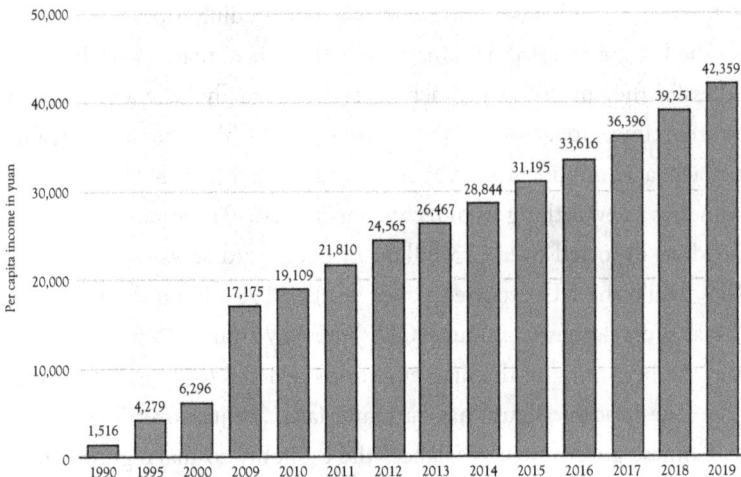

Source: Statista 2020

Annual Per Capita Disposable Income of Rural and Urban Households in China

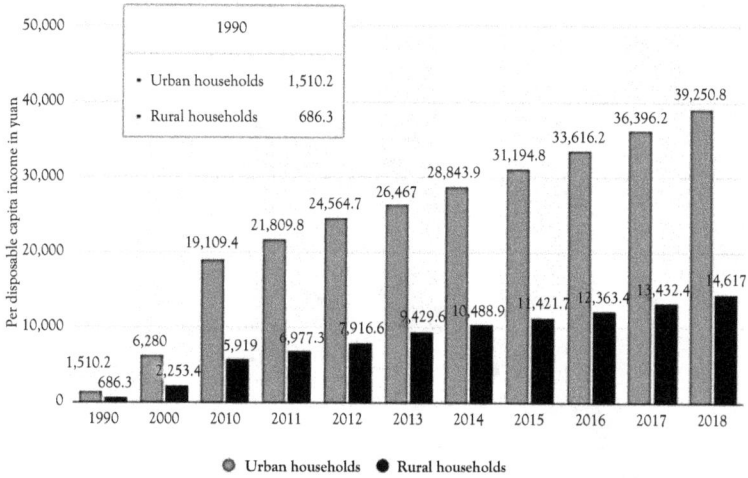

1990
- Urban households   1,510.2
- Rural households   686.3

Urban households   Rural households

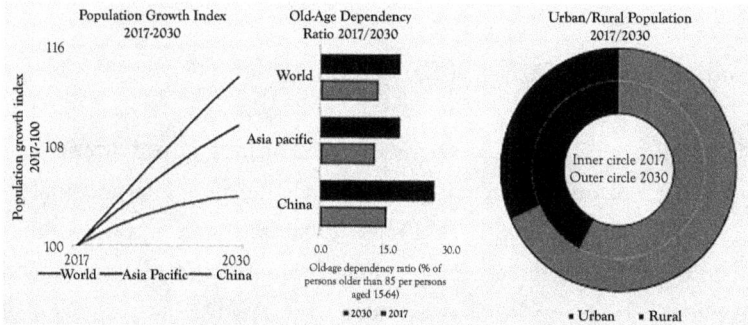

Population Growth Index 2017-2030

World ——Asia Pacific —— China

Old-Age Dependency Ratio 2017/2030

World
Asia pacific
China

0.0   15.0   30.0
Old-age dependency ratio (% of persons older than 85 per persons aged 15-64)

2030   2017

Urban/Rural Population 2017/2030

Inner circle 2017
Outer circle 2030

Urban   Rural

Source: Euromonitor International from national statisticsUN

Most Traded Goods Between U.S. & China

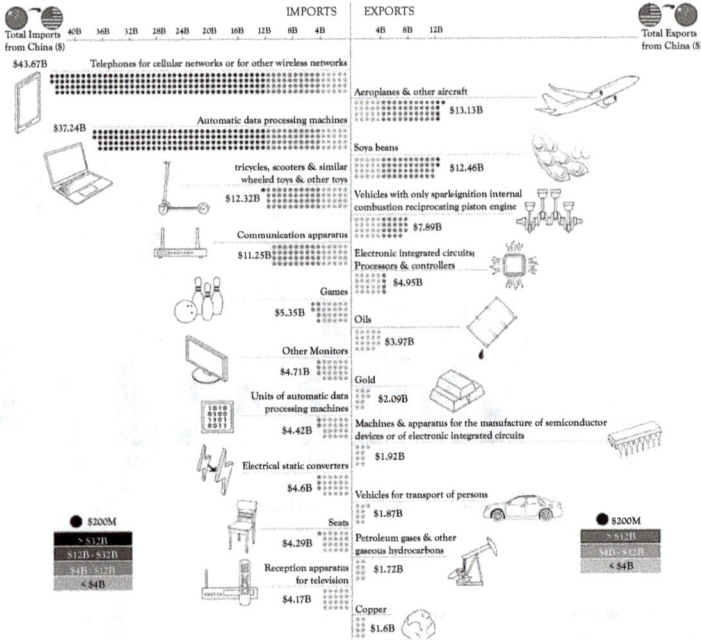

	IMPORTS	EXPORTS	
Total Imports from China ($)	40B 36B 32B 28B 24B 20B 16B 12B 8B 4B	4B 8B 12B	Total Exports from China ($)

$43.67B — Telephones for cellular networks or for other wireless networks

Aeroplanes & other aircraft $13.13B

$37.24B — Automatic data processing machines

Soya beans $12.46B

tricycles, scooters & similar wheeled toys & other toys $12.32B

Vehicles with only spark-ignition internal combustion reciprocating piston engine $7.89B

Communication apparatus $11.25B

Electronic integrated circuits; Processors & controllers $4.95B

Games $5.35B

Oils $3.97B

Other Monitors $4.71B

Gold $2.09B

Units of automatic data processing machines $4.42B

Machines & apparatus for the manufacture of semiconductor devices or of electronic integrated circuits $1.92B

Electrical static converters $4.6B

Vehicles for transport of persons $1.87B

$200M
> $32B
$12B - $32B
$4B - $12B
< $4B

Seats $4.29B

Petroleum gases & other gaseous hydrocarbons $1.72B

Reception apparatus for television $4.17B

$200M
> $12B
$4B - $12B
< $4B

Copper $1.6B

Source: Observatory of Economic Complexity

Meanwhile, rapid changes in transportation including road arteries and important rail improvements are increasing the economic potential of second- and third-tier cities. As rapid urbanization continues, China's urban population will keep on growing. It is estimated that one billion people will be living in cities by 2030. The steady volume growth of basic ingredients consumed by urban residents over the last two decades testifies to the increasing proportion of income spent on more frequent restaurant meals and prepackaged food. This urban sector of the Chinese market is therefore far more likely to be interested in new and imported products than consumers living in rural areas. China's major demographic changes will have major impacts on the country's economy and labor and consumer market, creating both opportunities and challenges for businesses. Factors contributing to these trends are various: population ageing, low birth and fertility rates (mostly due to China's one-child policy from 1979 to 2015), severe gender imbalance, rising wealth, and ongoing rural–urban labor migration.

Selling to China

Selling to China is selling to 1.4 billion consumers. It is well known that the most attractive feature of the Chinese market is its size.

Industry Sectors

The Food and Beverage Market in China

China has been the world's largest market for food and grocery retail since 2011, surpassing the United States. The Chinese food and beverage industry grew at an average annual rate of 30 percent. According to the Ministry of Commerce total retail sales are expected to grow 15 percent more annually in the next couple of years. China is currently the largest importer of food worldwide (after the European Union, the United States, and Japan). In terms of the origin of these food products the United States is currently the largest food exporter to China, followed by Brazil, Canada, Argentina, and Malaysia.

Despite the growing local competition and a fragmented distribution infrastructure, opportunities for Western businesses to sell their products in China are predicted to grow, driven by urbanization, increasing disposable income, an improving logistics infrastructure, a growing concern for food safety, and a growing trend for foreign foodstuffs. Highlighted opportunities for Western businesses in this sector include wine, dairy products, cheese, olive oil, sauces and tomato products, pasta, chocolate, high-end confectionery, finger food and snacks, coffee, breakfast cereal, and baby food. China's food and beverage imports have seen a strong growth in recent years. This phenomenon has been a significant factor in the overall strong growth of the Chinese grocery retail market.

Among the EU countries, France, Spain, the Netherlands, Germany, and Denmark are the top food exporters and the combined exports of these countries amount to more than 80 percent of the EU total exports. Wine exports make France the largest overall EU exporter of both food and beverages to China.

Food safety scandals remain prevalent in China. Incidents such as the tainted milk scandal or the dumping of contaminated pigs into the Huangpu River are still fresh in people's memories. Such scandals have undermined the trust and confidence in local food production processes and standards. Back in 2012, after it was revealed that KFC's Chinese suppliers used illegal drugs to fatten the chickens, the chain's sales plummeted in China. A 2020 Pew survey found that 43 percent of Chinese consumers are deeply concerned regarding food safety, especially after the coronavirus outbreak. These food safety incidents have had a huge impact on the purchase decisions of Chinese consumers. According to the same survey, more than 70 percent of consumers would consider stopping purchasing the brand if it was involved in a scandal. On the other hand, it is not only domestic companies that have come under fire over safety concerns. A few years ago, all milk powder from New Zealand was banned in China over concerns of botulism.

Despite these incidents, those who can afford would show preference for imported goods, particularly products for children. A 2020 survey revealed that over 60 percent of Chinese consumers would choose foreign brands if they could afford them, thus reflecting the low confidence in the domestic food industry. This complements the growing interest in imported organic food because there are also concerns regarding domestically certified organic products.

Market Structure

In China, imported food and beverages are generally consumed in city cafés, bars, hotels, and restaurants. Chinese consumers are increasingly showing their preference for Western-style food when they dine out. Many of the Western-style restaurants which were originally targeting expatriates now have a predominantly Chinese clientele. Many family celebrations and social occasions now take place in Western food restaurants. Imported food and beverages, being perceived as high-value goods, remain a status symbol in China. They are often used for display purposes. In this instance, packaging and branding are particularly important. As the gift-offering market remains an important tradition in Chinese culture, the wine industry is dominated by direct sales for gift-offering purposes. Such wines are individually presented in elegant gift boxes and usually accompanied by complementary gifts such as a pair of matching wine glasses.

Prepackaged snacks and finger food remain the most popular imported retail food products. They are packaged meals and range from Western-style biscuits to Asian-style meat and fish snacks. So far, apart from pasta and—to a lesser extent—cheese, Chinese consumers have shown few signs of taking Western food products home, which is largely due to the difference in local cooking methods and the abundance of regional cuisines.

Ovens are still uncommon, although they are increasing in popularity, especially small bench-top ovens. Baking, especially of biscuits and cakes, enjoys the greatest interest among Western cooking styles for Chinese consumers, a trend that benefits imported foodstuffs such as butter, flavoring and coloring products, and raising agents. However, Western-style dinner parties are not popular in China where entertaining and social occasions take place outside of the home and as a result there is little interest in Western upmarket dining and cooking paraphernalia.

As Chinese consumers experiment with unfamiliar foods outside the home, they are acquiring the taste for buying new ingredients in order that they may try out similar meals at home but this will only be on a small scale for simple meals. Retailers carry only small amounts of imported products, even in affluent cities.

Retail Chains

Convenience Stores

Imported food penetration tends to be relatively low among convenience store chains. In Shanghai several chains have shown interest but managements at these stores are usually unfamiliar with such products compared to their counterparts in the hypermarket sector. Due to limited storage and shelf space, convenience stores typically require regular restocking and smaller or single-serve packaging. However, foreign players such as FamilyMart and 7-Eleven are introducing more imported food products into their outlets. Smaller, privately owned convenience stores often carry imported packaged snacks, wine, and confectionery. These stores are more likely to see the value of high-margin imported food and often have better integrated distribution systems.

Supermarkets

The supermarket sector is fragmented in China and dominated by domestic players. Companies can be pretty successful in certain regions and nonexistent in others. Imported food products are relatively scarce in most local supermarkets because the price-sensitive working-class shoppers forming the consumer base of those stores are less inclined to buy new products than customers who frequent upscale stores and hypermarkets.

Hypermarkets

It is in hypermarkets where the majority of imported products find the greatest success. Hypermarkets are normally multifloor stores with extensive space offering a very wide variety of goods, including many nonfood items. International hypermarket retailers usually have a high level of familiarity with foreign brands and thus recognize the value of introducing imported products to the market. Such stores have favored distributors and generally avoid working with unfamiliar companies unless offered certain incentives and strong market support.

Specialty Supermarkets and Boutiques

Such stores are often adjacent to high-end department stores or upscale business centers, mainly in first- and second-tier cities, and usually stock large quantities of imported food products. This type of stores was originally designed for Western expatriates but is now becoming more popular among upper-middle-class Chinese consumers. Some of these companies have their own import and distribution teams, sourcing products directly from foreign suppliers. It is in fact through this type of outlets that high-end products first entered China, before actually expanding to hypermarkets and larger retail outlets.

Hotel and Restaurant Wholesalers

The high-end restaurant and hotel industry is an important gateway for Western products. Metro, a foreign company targeting small- and medium-sized restaurants has the largest selection of imported goods of any of the major international retailers. About 10 percent of their total sales revenue comes from imported products. For Metro, imported food has become one of their most important and successful business lines, with imported products accounting for 55 percent of the company's total Asia sales, which have seen an increase of 20 to 30 percent each year. The company has enhanced its sourcing center and import department and is determined to build direct links with Western manufacturers seeking to export to China.

Online

The online retail sector has seen a very rapid growth in recent years. China has the largest Internet population worldwide and it keeps growing in number. Out of the top 100 retail chains operating in China, 51 had established online stores by 2011. Online food and beverage delivery services supplying Western goods have already begun appearing in the market. Some of the most successful organic food suppliers began e-mail ordering around 2005 and have been offering home delivery service since 2007. These companies regularly supply households in Shanghai, Beijing, and restaurants in Shenzhen and Guangzhou. An increasing number of European wine suppliers are successfully selling their products in China's urban centers. Chinese consumers do trust recognizable Western websites, whom they believe supply genuine wine.

The Services Market in China

The development of the services sector in China had been constrained for decades by the country's focus on manufactured exports and the barriers to trade and investment in the services industry. China's services sector still accounts for a smaller percentage of GDP compared to the global average for developing countries. Nonetheless, China committed to a dramatic opening of the services sector after its accession to the World Trade Organization in 2001.

In the 13th Five Year Plan (FYP) 2016–2020, the Chinese government accorded strategic priority to the growth of the services sector and especially to the trade in services (TIS). It is in key services subsectors such as education, health care, finance, and logistics that China has decided to implement a more proactive opening-up strategy while the country also aims to rank among the top global exporters for tourism, transport, and construction, subsectors in which China has shown a comparative advantage. China not only aims at enlarging the scale of TIS but also at increasing its technological and knowledge intensity in order to improve international competitiveness.

To further encourage TIS growth the Chinese government is willing to accelerate the formulation of new regulations on promoting TIS while at the same time improving the legal and fiscal system for the services industry as a way to create an investment-friendly business environment.

The Technology Market in China

From genetically engineered rice to automation, advanced computing, cancer therapies, or fiber optics, China has approximately 600 million Internet users, almost twice the population of the United States. Although China's tech tycoons have outlined plans to enter foreign markets, most think the opportunities within China are too great to care too much about global expansion. Foreign companies seeking to enter this competitive market need to think about what value they can bring. Although gaming is not considered the fanciest business in the Silicon Valley it is the leading source of revenue for most tech companies. Advertising, the biggest source of revenue for mobile applications in the United States, is growing in China, but only represents 9 percent of Tencent's current revenue. The future profit potential will be to connect the phone with all sorts of offline businesses. The legacy taxi business is now threatened by people arranging car dispatches through their smartphones. Many existing businesses will be disrupted by the tech revolution, inviting new opportunities for companies to develop new products and services.

Opportunities and Challenges by Sector

This section discusses opportunities in the following industries:

- Food and beverage
- Pharmaceutical
- Environmental infrastructure
- Renewable energy
- Luxury goods
- Education
- TV and film

Food and Beverage

The Chinese F&B industry has been growing significantly over the past 15 years as incomes increase. Local production is not able to keep up with demand, which has resulted in China becoming a net importer of F&B products. In addition, the constant exposure of food safety issues of locally produced food has caused a great deal of public concern, leading to many consumers purchasing imported products when they can afford it. Therefore, there are significant opportunities for Western F&B companies from importing and distributing F&B products in the Chinese market to establishing joint ventures or Wholly Foreign Owned Enterprises (WFOEs).

Most Western foods in China are currently from the United States and benefit from ads and product placement in films and TV and the ubiquity of American culture. Nonetheless, even these products require extensive marketing and branding. EU products are much less easily known and understood and as Chinese consumers lack the knowledge on how to prepare them properly, they tend to be hesitant to buy such products. Therefore, a potential niche market of attractive and well-selected baskets of goods, accompanied with preparation and cooking instructions, exists.

Niche Markets

The F&B market is growing at a very fast rate but is mainly driven by price and is therefore dominated by low-cost local producers. The buoyant wine market set aside, other imported food and especially prepackaged products can expect to occupy only a small segment of the market, where novelty and quality win out over price.

POTENTIAL SEGMENTS	
Imported organic and natural products	This segment tends to represent health-conscious young parents shopping for their babies and family meals.
Gourmet foods	This segment is still a niche but is expanding to become a market in China. The concept of 'gourmet' often corresponds to products considered standard supermarket fare in Western countries.
High-end gifts	Packaging is paramount and margins tend to be pretty high in this segment. Gifts can be tailored to special events or Chinese celebrations offered by those who want to demonstrate their sophistication by presenting foreign gifts at traditional Chinese holidays. Gifts usually include chocolates, wine and high-end confectionery and packaged baked food.
Baskets of specialty western goods	Suitable goods for this segment include wine baskets, cheese, savory biscuits pre-packaged snack foods and preserved vegetables.

Western businesses can expect to find opportunities in variety of areas, including wine, dairy products, cheese, premium ice-cream, olives, tomato products, beer, high-end confectionery, breakfast cereal, prepackaged snacks and biscuits, coffee, frozen meat, seafood, as well as baby food.

Food

Frozen Meat and Seafood

The Opportunity

Every year China imports large quantities of meat and seafood (mainly fifth quarters and offals that Western consumers do not eat), which go mainly into the food services sector and processing facilities. In terms of fish, salmon from Scotland and Norway dominates the market in China and there are opportunities for Western companies to supply other varieties and species.

The Challenge

The F&B sector is facing two main challenges: mistrust of food safety and increasing costs. Increasing production costs (such as raw materials, labor, land, and transportation) are driving up food prices, with the additional cost being transferred to consumers for the most part. Additionally, protocol requirements and quarantine for frozen meat act as hurdles to the market. As a result, Hong Kong has often been the point of entry for seafood and meat products into the Chinese market through the so-called grey channel. Chinese authorities have recently put measures in order to stop this illegal importation and importers are now more interested in products that can be officially imported into China's main ports. Exporters are usually encouraged to confirm their products' eligibility to enter the Chinese market before engaging in commercial activities with any customers or directly investing in China business opportunities. Initial enquiries can be made to agriculture and quarantine authorities in their home country about this.

2018 imported food categories

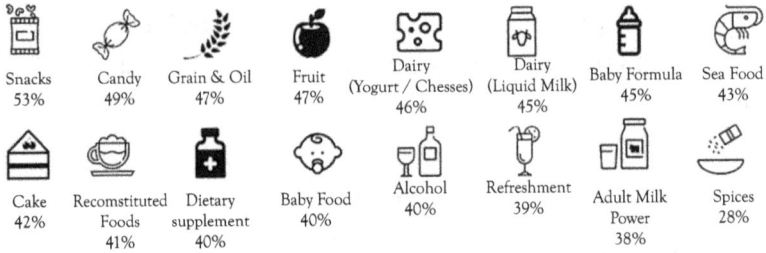

Snacks 53%	Candy 49%	Grain & Oil 47%	Fruit 47%	Dairy (Yogurt / Chesses) 46%
Dairy (Liquid Milk) 45%	Baby Formula 45%	Sea Food 43%		

Cake 42%	Recomstituted Foods 41%	Dietary supplement 40%	Baby Food 40%	Alcohol 40%
Refreshment 39%	Adult Milk Power 38%	Spices 28%		

Portrait of China's 'typical' imported food shopper

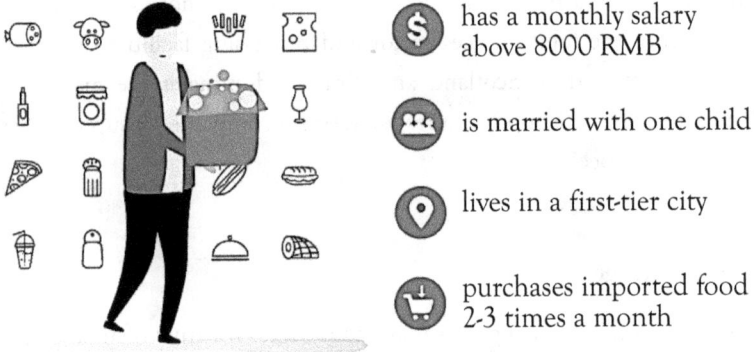

has a monthly salary above 8000 RMB

is married with one child

lives in a first-tier city

purchases imported food 2-3 times a month

Penetration rate of imported food and beverages in China (by category, %)

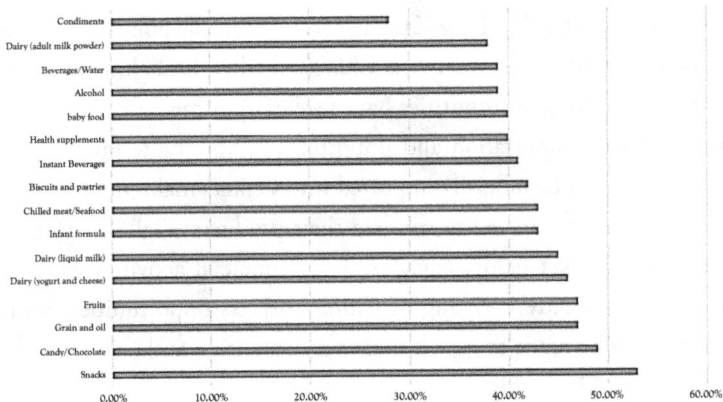

Condiments
Dairy (adult milk powder)
Beverages/Water
Alcohol
baby food
Health supplements
Instant Beverages
Biscuits and pastries
Chilled meat/Seafood
Infant formula
Dairy (liquid milk)
Dairy (yogurt and cheese)
Fruits
Grain and oil
Candy/Chocolate
Snacks

0.00%   10.00%   20.00%   30.00%   40.00%   50.00%   60.00%

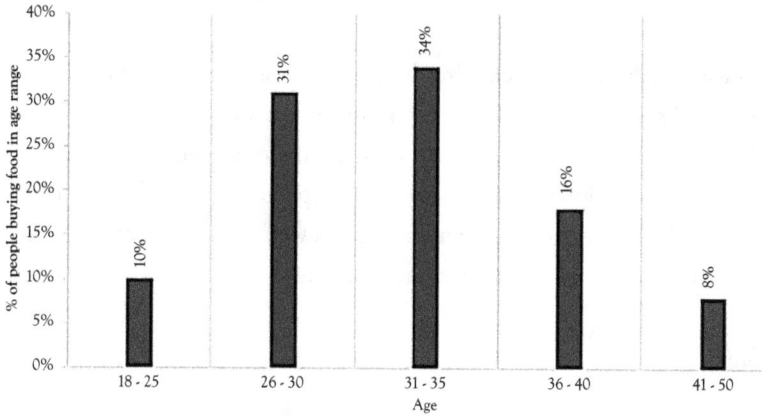

China's top 10 food import partners (by value, hundred million USD)

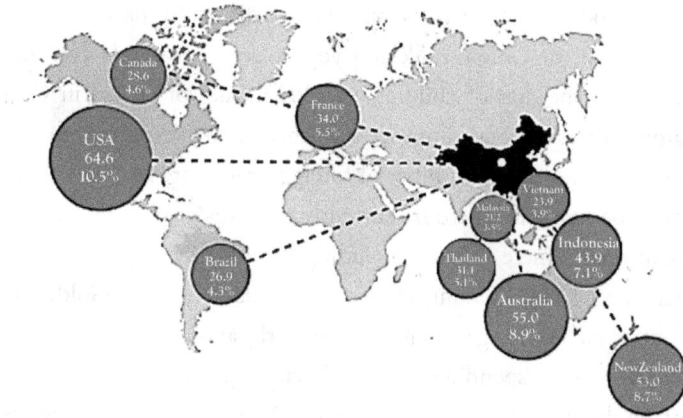

High-End Confectionery, Chocolate, and Prepackaged Snacks and Biscuits

The Opportunity

This market is growing rapidly as incomes keep rising. Prepackaged snack foods and high-end confectionery are popular for social occasions and now occupy extensive shelf space in Chinese stores and supermarkets.

The Challenge

Korean and Japanese snacks already represent a significant segment of the packaged snack food market. As in most international markets, however, China's market is dominated by local products at the lower end and Western confectionery products at the upper end. Imported products from both the United States and Europe as well as other Asian countries enjoy high brand recognition in the market.

Dairy

The Opportunity

According to recent industry statistics, total dairy sales in China reached 8.3 billion yuan ($1.1 billion) in 2019 and have seen a 25.14 percent increase since 2018. In fact, dairy products are among the most popular imported goods in China. Although not traditionally part of the diet in most regions of China, milk and yogurt are increasingly considered paramount to the diet of children. By 2023, sales of cheese in China, including processed and unprocessed cheese, are expected to reach $1.44 billion. A growing number of foreign brands are available in most Chinese supermarkets. There are currently more than 10 American cheese brands in the Chinese market, including AmeriDaily, Leprino, Borden, and Sargento. Other leading imported brands are Kerry Gold, Kraft, President, Feta, Suki, Bega, Laughing Cow, Arla, and Emmi. High-income households tend to spend a significantly larger proportion of the family income on dairy products, which represent 21.3 kilos per capita per year, than low-income household where dairy product consumption represents no more than 6.98 kilos per capita per year, thus placing dairy products in the category of high-end products for those with large disposable income. In addition, domestic food safety scandals and rising concern over the domestic dairy industry have created a rapidly growing demand for high-quality, safe, and reliable products, especially from overseas markets.

The Challenge

Cold-chain distribution networks remain pretty much underdeveloped across China and distrust of local dairy products has encouraged the use of nontariff barriers, including strict sanitary requirements, in an attempt to protect local production.

Pasta, Sauces, and Olive Oil

The Opportunity

These foods resonate with Chinese consumers, since the Western versions have been present in fast-food chains for a few decades now. Consumers are far more familiar with these foods than with other novelty "gourmet" products.

The Challenge

In spite of the familiarity, the market remains small for these items, meaning that even small profit margins require high-volume sales.

Beverages

Beer

The Opportunity

China's beer market grew by almost 30 percent in volume between 2006 and 2011 and, according to Mitel, the total consumption volume was 50 billion liters. Opportunities for boutique drinks such as beer and soft drinks are currently available through local distribution channels to bars and specialist stores in large cities. For the dedicated beer enthusiast, microbreweries are mushrooming and opportunities arise in second-tier cities as well, although this requires residency in China.

Light beers are normally preferred and some EU brewers have developed beers specifically for the Chinese market. Traditional celebrations are very popular and offer opportunities to promote boutique beers and drinks to Chinese.

The Challenge

The Chinese beer market is now the biggest in the world. However, even large international brands have found it very hard to survive, while smaller ones compete in a never-ending search for economies of scale, with their production based in China. Distribution, quality control, and hygiene are the main challenges in this market. Because of the relative price inelasticity in comparison with the Chinese market and the low price of local beer, competition stays high.

Wine

The Opportunity

China was the largest wine importing country in whole Asia in 2020 and mainland China imported more than US $800 million that year. Wine-exporting countries such as France, Italy, Australia, the United States, Chile, and South Africa have had a strong China presence for years. New brands of various origins find ways into Chinese households each year. Wine constitutes the largest EU export to China by a large margin. Wine is very successfully marketed in China as a healthy alternative to Chinese baijiu (white spirit). Far from being a luxury, wine is China's way of illustrating social status.

The Challenge

Exorbitantly priced, chemically altered, and counterfeit wines flush the market. Few effective government supervision measures combined with lack of consumer wine experience mean that genuine wine-sellers are forced to police the market themselves. For instance, a large EU wine and spirit producer employs staff exclusively to identify counterfeits and mount legal challenges. Very cheap wine (RMB 20–58) and wine for the high-end gift market (RMB 1,500) have a reasonably ready market, but mid-range quality wines (RMB 100–300) are hard to sell to Chinese consumers without expensive wine-tastings and other marketing activities.

	Food			Beverages	
	Chocolate, high-end confectionery, pre-packaged biscuits and snacks	Dairy	Pasta, Pasta sauces and Olive Oil	Wine	Beer
Opportunities Across the Board	• Growing urban middle class. • Dining out at hotels, restaurants, cafes and bars is a huge growth area.. • Propensity for using western F&B products as gifts. • Continued market potential in first tier cities and growing markets in second and third tiers.				
Opportunities	• Demand growing as incomes increases. • Pre-packaged snack foods and confectionery are popular for entertaining.	• Amongst the most popular imported products. • Food safety crises leading to preference for foreign products.	• has resonance with Chinese consumers.	• The largest EU export to china. • Potential in second and third tier cities.	• Opportunities for boutique beers. • Opportunities in second-tier cities.
Challenges Across the Board	• Cultural hurdles - On the whole, Chinese tastes and kitchens not yet ready for full adoption of western foods. • Increasing local competition. • Fragmented localised distribution channels. • Cold-chain storage under developed.				
Challenges	• Strong Japanese and Korean competition in snacks industry • US confectionery dominant at the upper and lower ends.	• Cold-chain distribution networks • Non-tariff barriers.	• Small profit margins require high volume sales.	• Countries wines flush the market. • Lack of consumer wine experience. • Mid-range quality wines are difficult to sell.	• Quality control, hygiene and distribution.
Legal Barriers		• Distribution of food is subject to the licensing system in China. Companies engaging in distribution have to apply for the food distribution licence. • Manufacturers of certain imported food (for instance meat products) have to be registered with the Certification and Accreditation Administration (CNCA).		• Distribution of beverages is subject to the licensing system in China. Companies engaging in distribution of beverage have to apply for the food distribution licence. • Distributors of alcohol products must be filed with the local bureau of commerce.	
Taxes	• Corporation tax 25%. • VAT 17% / 13%. • City Maintenance and Construction Tax 1 - 7% of the VAT depending on location. • Education surcharge 3% of the VAT.				
Standard, Certification and Labelling requirements	• Sanitary certification is issued by the local quarantine bureau (CIQ) and based on products sample inspection. • Chinese national (GB) standards and professionals standards covering the technical quality and safety (hygiene) requirement, including food additives. • Labelling requirements for food, beverage and food for special dietary must be provided in chinese; lable must be verified by the local quarantine bureau.				

Pharmaceuticals

China's pharmaceutical market has been constantly growing in recent years and is estimated to reach $161.8 billion by 2023, taking a 30 percent share of the global market. China's pharmaceutical market is highly fragmented, with the top 10 players accounting for only 25 percent of the market. Among these players, almost half are foreign companies. Shanghai, Jiangsu, Zhejiang, and Guangdong are key locations where large pharmaceutical groups cluster.

In 2009, the Chinese government launched a Healthcare Reform Plan aiming to build up a comprehensive national health care system by 2020. From 2009 to 2011, the first stage of the reform was implemented in which basic medical insurance (BMI) was provided to 95 percent of the population. In addition, health care services have improved while the average price of basic pharmaceutical products decreased by around 30 percent.

The expanded coverage of BMI is expected to further drive higher demand for pharmaceuticals in China. Additional drivers include an already large aging population (the country is expected to have 350 million people over 65 by 2050), a growing middle class, and an ongoing health care reform. Opportunities exist in various subsectors such as over-the-counter (OTC), biomedicine, prescription drugs, and equipment related to R&D drug manufacturing. On the other hand, the regulatory environment can be challenging for most Western companies, which explains why it is important to understand how China's regulations pertain to their products or services.

Top 10 Chinese Pharma Companies
2018 Revenues (USD Billions)

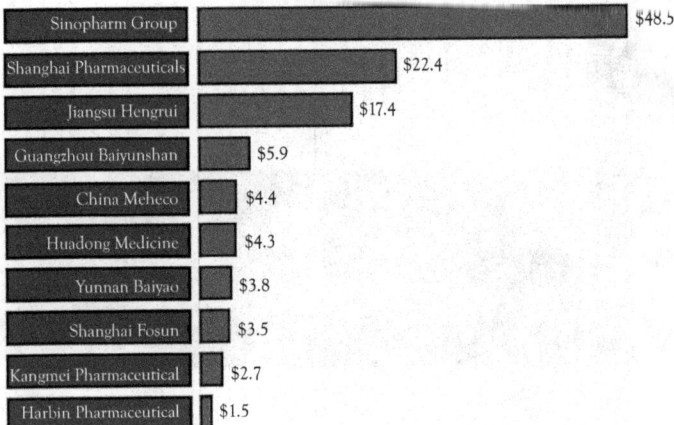

Company	Revenue
Sinopharm Group	$48.5
Shanghai Pharmaceuticals	$22.4
Jiangsu Hengrui	$17.4
Guangzhou Baiyunshan	$5.9
China Meheco	$4.4
Huadong Medicine	$4.3
Yunnan Baiyao	$3.8
Shanghai Fosun	$3.5
Kangmei Pharmaceutical	$2.7
Harbin Pharmaceutical	$1.5

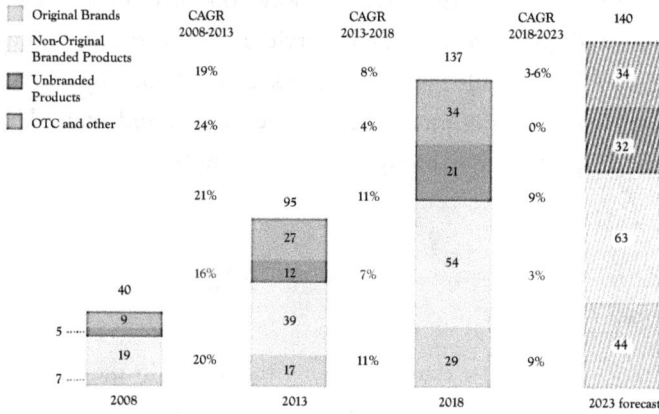

CHINA SPENDING 2008-2023 AND COMPOUND ANNUAL GROWTH CONSTANT USD Bn

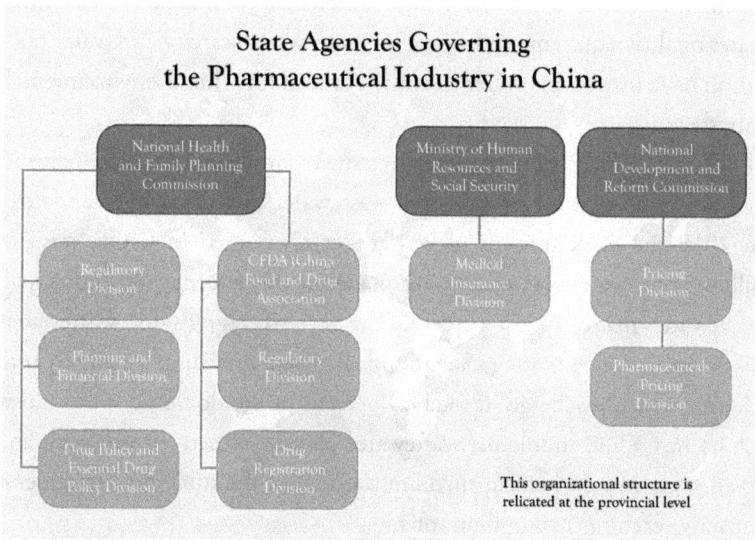

State Agencies Governing the Pharmaceutical Industry in China

This organizational structure is relicated at the provincial level

Environmental Infrastructure

China has undergone massive industrial and urbanization development over the last three decades. This growth has been coupled with significant challenges in regard to environmental protection. China has some of the world's most polluted cities, lakes, and rivers. Investment in pollution treatment exceeds U.S. $8 billion and most of it is in waste gas (47 percent) and wastewater treatment (35 percent).

Companies will find both opportunities and challenges in China's environmental infrastructure sector. Key opportunities include technology and plant management services. On the other hand, there are significant challenges in the market mainly because the key global players are already established in the market and many large infrastructure projects go through a rather nontransparent bidding process.

Wastewater Treatment

China's water resource per capita is among the lowest in the world. In addition, there is severe regional water imbalance as about 80 percent of the water supply is in the south with northern and western China experiencing droughts. Only 61 percent of China's largest watersheds reach the water quality requirements of type III; both water scarcity and water pollution have made wastewater treatment crucial for China's environmental infrastructure.

China's municipal wastewater treatment rate has reached 83 percent and about 95 percent of industrial wastewater met discharge standards. In 2018 the total amount of wastewater discharged in China was 70 billion tons, industrial wastewater made up 38 percent, and municipal wastewater made up 63 percent. The top six regions for wastewater discharge are Guangdong, Shandong, Jiangsu, Zhejiang, Guangxi, and Henan, which discharge in total 44 percent of the domestic wastewater. China has 3,508 municipal wastewater plants, 72 percent of which are small sized and 20 percent medium sized, with the total daily treatment capacity reaching 140 million tons.

Despite the increasing number of wastewater treatment plants and increasing treatment capacity, the current volume of treated wastewater is much lower than the designed treatment capacity. Municipal wastewater treatment growth has been limited due to insufficient piping networks, insufficient operational funds, and so on. For example, because the length of the piping network in Jilin is only 35 percent of that designed, three wastewater treatment plants are not operating.

Top Six Provinces for Wastewater Discharge

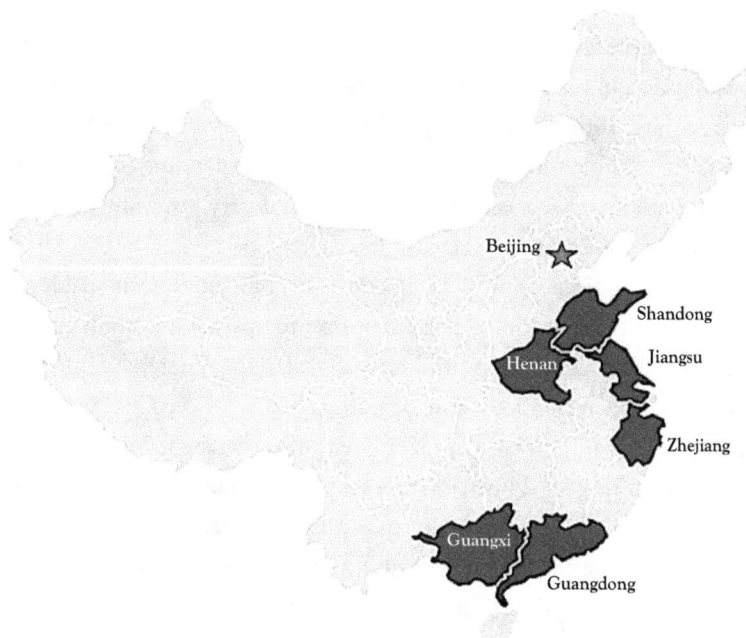

Source: JLI Analysis on multiple sources

The Chinese government invested more than U.S. $71 billion in municipal wastewater treatment and another U.S. $68 billion in industrial wastewater in the period from 2011 to 2015. The four main focal areas for investment include water reclamation; wastewater treatment facilities; sludge treatment, disposal, and piping network; and construction. About 40 percent of companies in this sector are foreign invested and engage mainly in providing integrated wastewater treatment services and advanced technology. Key international players include Suez, Veolia, and Dais, while major domestic players include Beijing Capital Group, Shenzhen Water Group, and Tianjin Capital Environment Protection Co.

Solid Waste Treatment

China is the largest country in the world in terms of solid waste generation, with total solid waste currently exceeding three billion tons. Industrial waste accounts for 95 percent of solid waste, with the remainder being municipal waste. The rate for industrial solid waste exceeds 70 percent.

Renewable Energy

China has become the leader worldwide in terms of installed capacity and consumption of renewable energy, with wind power capacity accounting for one-third of the world's total and solar power capacity accounting for one-fourth. China still faces a lot of challenges in expanding its renewable energy. Rather than market forces driving the industry, government targets on installed capacity are the key drivers of clean energy. In addition, many government projects tend to favor domestic companies, thus making it more difficult for foreign-owned enterprises to operate in certain sectors. On the other hand, opportunities still exist for Western companies with advanced technology and operational experience. China's energy consumption has been growing at an average yearly rate of 7 percent since 2011, accounting for 24 percent of world's energy consumption in 2020. It is equally interesting to notice that nonfossil energy (including solar power, hydropower, wind power, and biofuels) accounts for less than 8 percent of China's primary energy consumption.

China energy generation, 2019

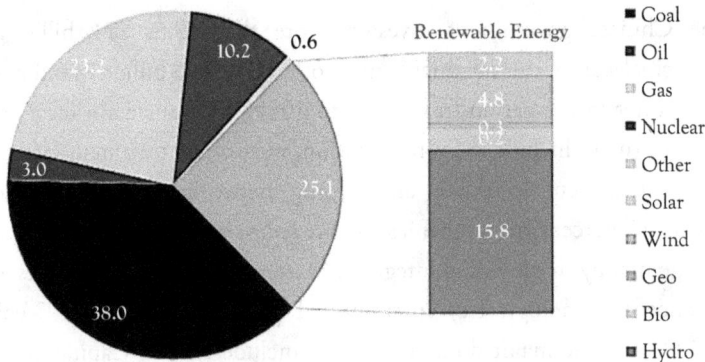

Source: BP, Statistical Review of World Energy 2019

The Belt and Road initiative is a China-led effort—backed by the United Nations—to promote economic development and inter-regional connectivity in more than 155 countries and is the largest single investment in infrastructure in generations. It was announced in 2013 by the Chinese government as a project to expand the ancient trade routes across six economic corridors, stretching through three continents.

This undertaking involves trillions of dollars of investment, especially in energy, technology, transportation, industrial capacity, telecommunications infrastructure, and technical capacity building. At the same, China's 13th Five Year Plan 2016 to 2020 has set the target for 15 percent share of primary energy to come from renewable sources, aiming to reduce carbon intensity of GDP by 50 percent by 2025. The mid-long-term development plan for renewable energy aims to increase solar power installed capacity to 20 to 30 GW (gigawatts), hydropower to 300 GW, wind power to 150 GW, and biomass power to 30 GW by 2020.

Overview of China's renewable energy market, 2019

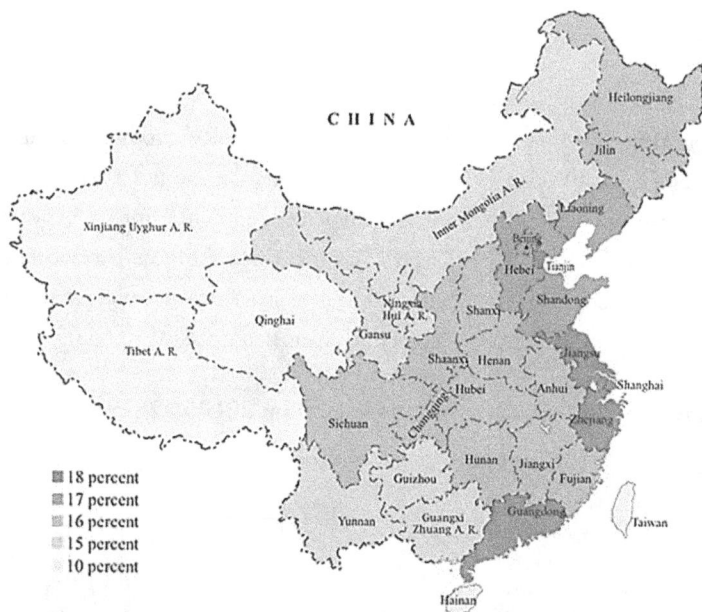

CHINA

Heilongjiang
Jilin
Liaoning
Xinjiang Uyghur A. R.
Inner Mongolia A. R.
Beijing
Hebei Tianjin
Shandong
Ningxia Hui A. R.
Shanxi
Qinghai
Gansu
Shaanxi Henan
Jiangsu
Hubei Anhui Shanghai
Chongqing Zhejiang
Sichuan
Hunan Jiangxi
Guizhou Fujian
Yunnan Guangxi Zhuang A. R. Guangdong Taiwan
Tibet A. R.
Hainan

- 18 percent
- 17 percent
- 16 percent
- 15 percent
- 10 percent

Source: Asia Briefing analysis, based on Deutsche Bank data

China has spent more on clean energy infrastructure than the United States and the European Union combined. The developing trends across the renewable energy industry in China in 2019 show that hydropower remains the dominant energy source in China's renewable energy system, followed by wind, and that hydropower remains the dominant energy source in the country's renewable energy system, followed by wind and solar energy. Geothermal and biomass power capacity have also been growing in recent years, albeit at a much slower pace.

According to Shi Yubo, former vice administrator of China's National Energy Administration (NEA) and current executive vice chairman of the China Energy Research Society, China's installed wind power capacity doubled from 2016 to 2020, from 96 to 184 GW, while installed PV capacity tripled from 25 to 174 GW during the same period. Based on this pace of growth, investment in renewable energy has a promising future. Despite the country's huge demand for fossil fuels, investment in low-carbon power generation and clean energy technologies is expected to exceed U.S. $6 trillion over the next 20 years.

Solar PV

China is currently the largest manufacturer of solar PV, with its production accounting for almost 50 percent of global solar PV production. About 90 percent of PV panels are exported. There are about 1,000 solar PV companies in China with more than 60 percent of them being concentrated around the Yangtze River Delta. The top three Chinese producers are GCL, Suntech, and Trina Solar while key international players include First Solar (United States), Motech (Taiwan), and CSI (Canada).

Cumulative photovoltaic installations from 2010 to 2019

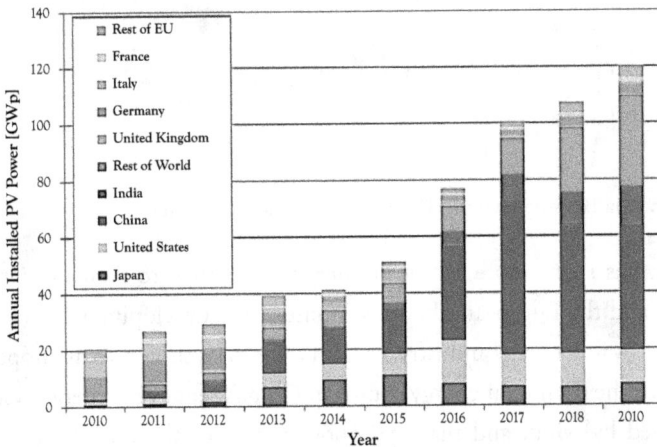

Source: Solar Power Europe 2019, Photovoltaic Energy Barometer 2019, own analysis

Cumulative installed capacity of wind Power worldwide in 2019, by country (in megawatts)*

Country	Capacity
China	2,37,029
United States	1,05,433
Germany	61,357
India**	37,529
Spain	25,808
United Kingdom	23,515
France	16,646
Brazil	15,452
Canada	13,413
Rest of the world	10,512

Cumulative installed capacity in megawatts

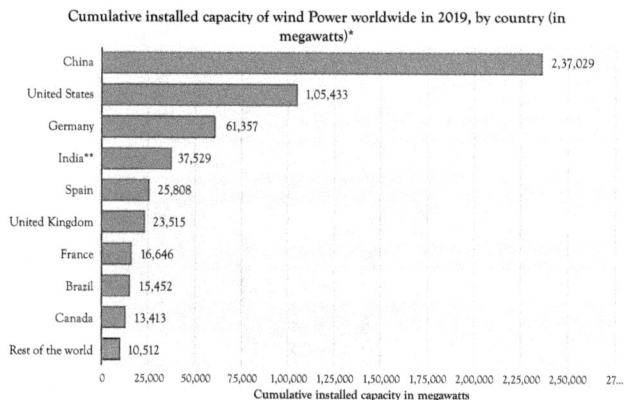

Source: GWEC © Statista 2020

Wind Power

China's wind power installed capacity is ranked number one worldwide. About 80 percent of exploitable wind power resources are concentrated in north China (Hebei and Inner Mongolia), northeast China (Jilin, Heilongiang, and Liaoning), and northwest China (Qinghai, Gansu, Xinjiang, Tibet, etc.). China's largest wind farm operators include Datang Renewable, Longyuan Power, and Huaneng Renewables. Iberola is the world's largest wind farm operator and has invested in China's wind power fields since 2006. China has evolved into the largest wind turbine market in the world. The three largest domestic manufacturers of wind turbines include Sinovel, Dongfang, and Goldwind while key international players include Gamesa (Spain), GE (United States), Vestas (Denmark), Siemens, and Suzlon (India). The wind turbine blade segment is very concentrated with around 80 domestic and international manufacturers, including Mitsubishi (Japan), LM (Netherlands), and AVIC Huiteng.

Biomass Power

Biomass power is still relatively nascent in China and the major biomass resources are concentrated in the rural areas of the country. The total number of biomass power companies totally exceeds 200 and includes key players such as Natural Bioenergy, Kaidi Electric, CECIC, and Natural Bio Energy, as well as Top Resource Conservation and Guangdong Shaoneng. Many international companies have started showing interest

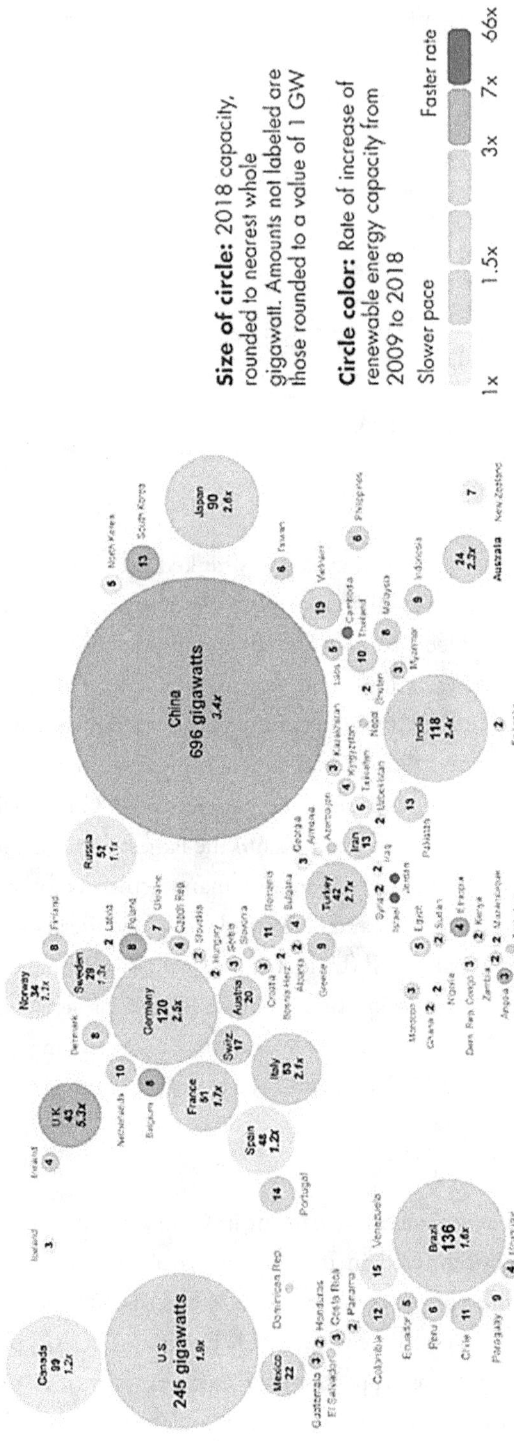
Size of circle: 2018 capacity, rounded to nearest whole gigawatt. Amounts not labeled are those rounded to a value of 1 GW
Circle color: Rate of increase of renewable energy capacity from 2009 to 2018
Slower pace
Faster rate
1x
1.5x
3x
7x
66x
China
696 gigawatts
3.4x
U.S.
245 gigawatts
1.9x
Brazil
136
1.6x
Germany
120
2.5x
India
118
2.4x
Canada
99
1.2x
Japan
90
2.6x

in China's biomass power market. For example, Future NRG, a company from Malaysia, invested U.S. $42 million in its first wholly owned biomass power project in Shangdong a few years ago. However, lack of raw materials, capital, and talent are key challenges for the development of biomass power in China.

The State Of Global Renewable Energy Employment

Number of employees in the renewable energy sector in 2018 (selected countries)

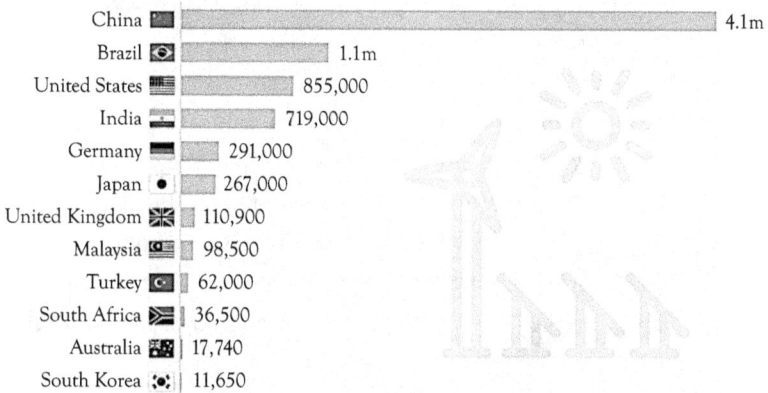

Country	Employees
China	4.1m
Brazil	1.1m
United States	855,000
India	719,000
Germany	291,000
Japan	267,000
United Kingdom	110,900
Malaysia	98,500
Turkey	62,000
South Africa	36,500
Australia	17,740
South Korea	11,650

Source: International Renewable Energy Agency

Renewable energy capacity investment by country, 2010 to the first half of 2019, in USD billions:

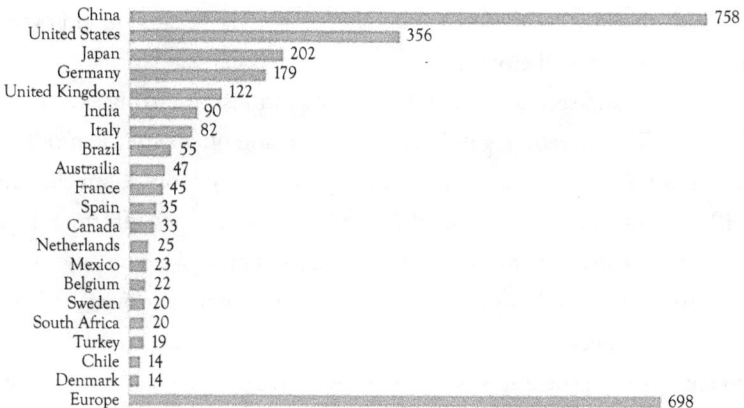

China	758
United States	356
Japan	202
Germany	179
United Kingdom	122
India	90
Italy	82
Brazil	55
Austrailia	47
France	45
Spain	35
Canada	33
Netherlands	25
Mexico	23
Belgium	22
Sweden	20
South Africa	20
Turkey	19
Chile	14
Denmark	14
Europe	698

Source: Global Trends in Renewable Energy Investment 2019, based on data from BloombergNEF

Luxury Goods

China's luxury market has been developing very rapidly in recent years and has a very different consumer profile than many other markets in that the majority of luxury consumers are below the age of 45. China's luxury industry is expected to remain strong in the next 10 years and accounts for almost 20 percent of global sales for luxury products. The majority of luxury goods sales are concentrated mainly in Beijing, Shanghai, Jiangsu, Guangdong, and Zhejiang. These provinces are highly developed markets and account for 65 percent of total luxury sales in China. On the other hand, these markets are saturated and competition is pretty high as most luxury brands have already established their presence there. As a result, many major brands have begun expanding into developing provinces such as Sichuan, Yunnan, and Chongqing to secure larger market shares. Brands such as Cartier, Louis Vuitton, Rolex, Chanel, and Rolex already have a strong presence in the Chinese market, having entered through direct stores and an expansive dealer network.

Given that developed markets are already saturated and competition is fierce in most product categories, luxury brands are penetrating the developing provinces. Brand awareness is so important in China and can take many years to build if a brand is not known internationally. An example is Tiffany & Co. which is a relatively recent entrant into the Chinese market. The brand has done well though, because brand awareness was high even before the company entered China.

In first- and second-tier cities, key motivations for buying such goods include self-pampering, gaining recognition, and quality of the products, while in third- and fourth-tier cities, key drivers are more about showing off. Consumers interested in this product category get information in premium magazines or online (e.g., official brand websites and social web tools such as Weibo). At the same time, purchasing overseas is not uncommon because prices tend to be lower than in China, mainly due to taxes that can be in excess of 40 percent. In addition, there are a larger variety of product offerings abroad, which explain the recent trend among Chinese consumers to travel to Hong Kong, Europe, or the United States to purchase luxury goods.

Global personal-luxury-goods[1]
market evolution, RMB[2] billion

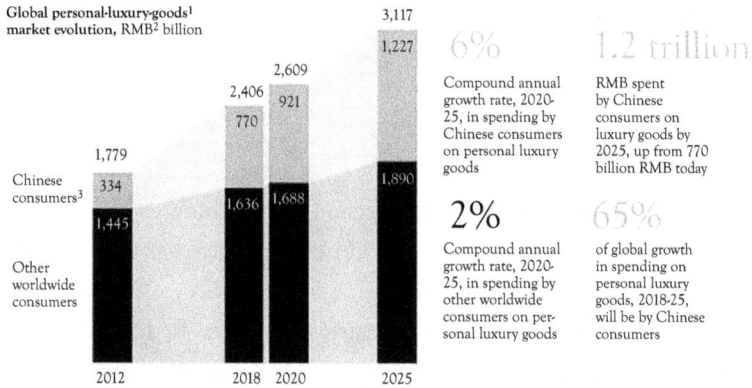

6%

Compound annual growth rate, 2020-25, in spending by Chinese consumers on personal luxury goods

1.2 trillion

RMB spent by Chinese consumers on luxury goods by 2025, up from 770 billion RMB today

2%

Compound annual growth rate, 2020-25, in spending by other worldwide consumers on personal luxury goods

65%

of global growth in spending on personal luxury goods, 2018-25, will be by Chinese consumers

1. Ready to wear, accessories, watches and jewelry, and beauty.
2. Fixed exchange rate of €1 - 7.3 RMB.
3. Both domestic and overseas spending.

Source: China Luxury Report 2019, China Luxury Report 2017

**Global personal luxury goods market evolution
(billion RMB)**

■ Chinese consumers   ▧ Other worldwide consumers

% of Chinese consumers   19%   32%   35%   40%

Source: McKinsey China Report 2019, WalktheChat Analysis

Education

The market value of the education industry has been growing at an average rate of 12 percent since 2009 per annum in China. In 2019, private education accounts for around 44 percent of the entire industry and has been growing at a 15 percent rate every year since 2009. The central government has emphasized education as a pillar industry with a stated goal of increasing government spending on education to 4 percent of the total national GDP. In addition the government implemented the National Mid-to-Long-Term Education Reform and Development Plan from 2010 to 2020 which has driven further the industry through to the next decade.

Preschool Education

The limited number of public preschools and kindergartens cannot meet the demands of the 110 million children aged 0 to 6, among which around 10 percent are urban children aged 0 to 3. Currently, key private preschools and kindergartens include Red Yellow Blue Education (Beijing), Etonkids (Beijing), Great Man (Hong Kong), S&S Worldwide (United States), Color-Me (United States), and Montessori (Italy).

Primary and Secondary Education

The number of primary schools has decreased by more than 60 percent from 629,000 to 243,000 in 2020, while secondary schools decreased by about 20 percent from 66,000 to 54,000 over the same period. A large number of these schools were closed because of their inability to compete in terms of educational products, teaching resources, and services.

Higher Education

Higher education is facing pressure from the decreasing number of applicants, a phenomenon due to China's one-child policy and the increasing number of Chinese students applying for education overseas. Chinese students enrolled by American academic colleges and universities increased by 26 percent from just 106,000 to almost 134,000 only from 2010 to 2011. Since then, more than 800 Sino-foreign academic joint ventures and joint education programs have been approved such as Shanghai Jiao Tong University SJTU-UM Joint Institute, established by SJTU and the University of Michigan (United States).

With the increasing spending on education and regulatory support of the central and local governments, especially in central and western China, there are many opportunities for Western companies in many segments, not only in preschool and vocational education but also in joint education programs. First-tier cities in eastern China maintain an attractive—and still—competitive market.

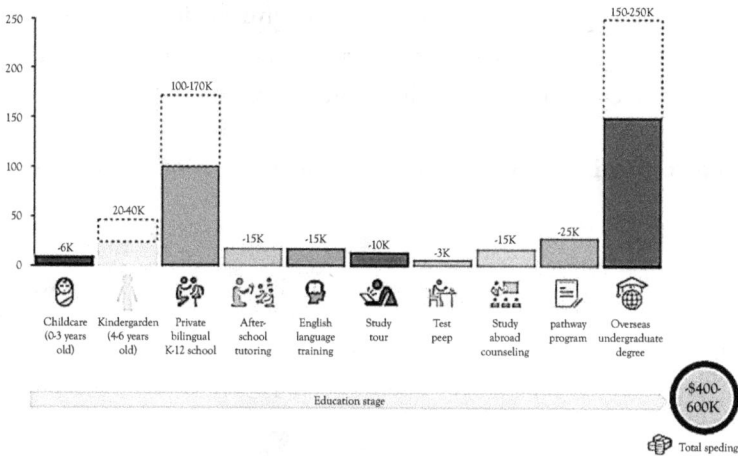

Childcare (0-3 years old)	Kindergarden (4-6 years old)	Private bilingual K-12 school
-6K	20-40K	100-170K

Education stage — Total speding — -$400-600K

Estimated spending of affluent parents on a child's education, by education stage

The desire of Chinese for premium products does not solely apply to consumer goods. Approximately 50 percent of Chinese consumers report they will "always buy the most expensive product across categories." What was ordinarily a trend across in the top segment of society two decades ago is now considered a social norm, affecting consumer behavior and giving rise to new luxury sectors, such as boutique education. The private education market in China is booming and had reached U.S. $330 billion in 2020. This growth is not occurring only in terms of quantity of education but also in terms of quality. With an increasingly affluent urban and cosmopolitan population and the world's longest period of sustained economic growth, Chinese parents are turning to private education at an unprecedented rate.

The demand for quality education is driven by three factors: an increasing international outlook, seeking advantage in hypercompetitive fields, and a strong preference for premium branded goods. Combined, these factors have led to continuous and sustainable growth in this sector. An increase in demand for private education has also led to an increase in quality and availability.

Driven by the consumer desire for world-class education, private schools that offer English language and bilingual education are filling a gap that the state does not provide. Outside of official schooling, parents are spending big on other forms of education to give children a competitive edge, including after-school tutoring, private language and music courses, study abroad counseling, and pathway programs.

Market capitalization of the 15 largest listed education companies

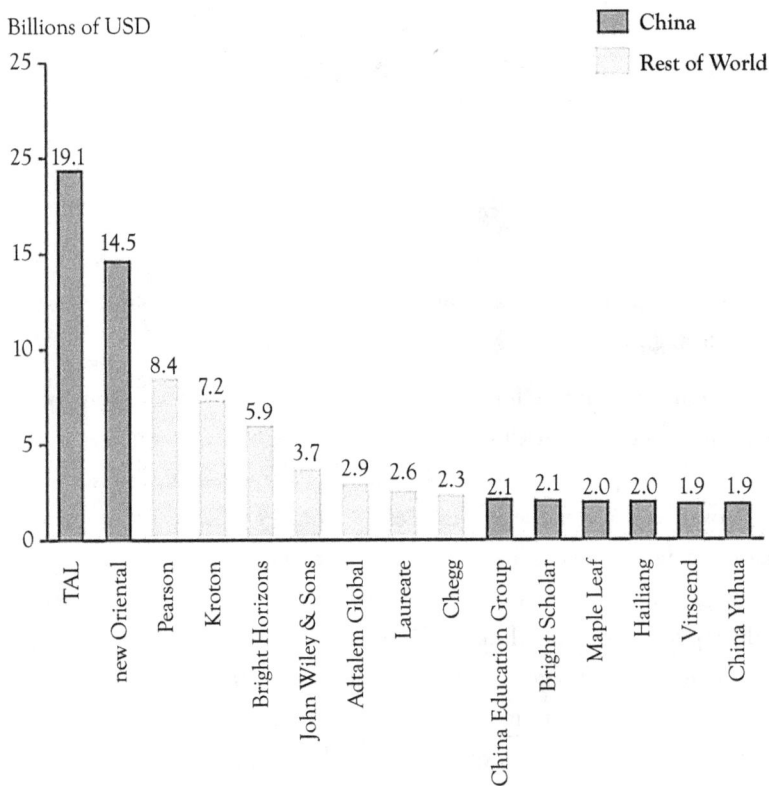

Billions of USD

China

Rest of World

25

25 — 19.1

15 — 14.5

10 —

8.4

7.2

5.9

5 —

3.7

2.9   2.6   2.3   2.1   2.1   2.0   2.0   1.9   1.9

0 —

TAL · new Oriental · Pearson · Kroton · Bright Horizons · John Wiley & Sons · Adtalem Global · Laureate · Chegg · China Education Group · Bright Scholar · Maple Leaf · Hailiang · Virscend · China Yuhua

Affluent parents in China spend more than double that of their counterparts in other similar emerging economies. The difference is significant, especially taking into account the fact that Chinese households have one or two children less than most Western families. The sheer amount of competition to access top universities in China as well as abroad is one of the fundamental factors driving growth. The Chinese are beginning to dominate the transnational education market, making up about 20 percent of the global marketplace. This is creating a big shift in the Chinese mindset, as students increasingly search for foreign elements in their traditional education. This growing international outlook is having an effect on the types of education offered, with international schools and premium K–12 schools teaching courses of the national curriculum in English.

Looking toward the future, the education sector will continue to grow substantially, attracting more investments and adapting to the desires of the modern Chinese learner. With China going global, private education operators are likely to develop unique and exportable techniques. Armed with local experience, homegrown companies will look outside of China for opportunities.

TV and Film

The government has strict control on all forms of media in China and as a result the TV and film industry is highly regulated. The government is also focusing on growing the domestic industry through use of various policies which are often considered protectionist. For example, targets are set for the percentage of revenues generated by domestic versus imported films. In addition, the government provides incentives for the development of domestic technology, such as the Chinese version of IMAX. There is, however, significant potential in China's TV and film industries as the number of screens and the country's TV audience base continue to grow. Opportunities for Western companies may be found in coproducing films, in postproduction of films, or in other TV technologies.

China has a TV audience of 1.4 billion people and the country's broadcast coverage, especially in rural parts, continues to grow. Broadcasting revenues have seen a 30 percent year-on-year growth over the last years, with advertising revenues making up nearly 40 percent of the total profit. The State Administration of Radio, Film and Television (SARFT) regulates and censors films, TV shows, and commercials. Although the content allowed on Chinese TV was liberalized after China's entry into the WTO in 2001, even today allowable content must not be politically inappropriate or sensitive. Furthermore, foreign investment is not allowed to exceed 49 percent in any company in China's TV industry.

China Central Television (CCTV), Shanghai Media Group (SMG), and Hunan Broadcasting System (HBS) are by far the largest broadcasting companies in terms of revenue, while foreign satellite TV channels such as BBC, CNN, or MTV are only able to enter China after obtaining broadcasting landing rights. Given that in the past decade Internet usage has grown significantly to 600 million users, younger generation audiences lean toward new media mobile TV. However, traditional TV remains the leading media outlet mainly due to the large audience base.

There is a general demand for American TV dramas, especially in first- and second-tier cities, where audiences tend to be more open to Western culture. On the other hand, because of a strict censorship process it can take an average of 2 years or even longer before Chinese audiences are able to see American dramas on TV. Therefore, such dramas are mostly viewed online or via pirated DVDs.

Films

In its Five Year Plan, the Chinese government expressed plans to promote the culture industry by promoting its value with an annual growth rate of 15 percent. The domestic film market is also regulated by SARTF, which regulates and censors the content of all movies that are released in China. Foreign companies are restricted in film production and distribution in China and only representative offices are allowed to be established. There is also a quota on the number of foreign films imported into China but this quota is expected to be increased or even cancelled in the future. China Film Import and Export Company, a subsidiary of China Film Group, is the only authorized company to import films.

The film market is dominated by several large domestic players, such as Huayi Brothers, China Film Group, and Polybona, with such companies engaged in the entire supply chain and in charge of production, distribution, and exhibition. The most common way for foreign players to enter this market is through importing films or through engaging in joint production. American films currently dominate the market in terms of foreign films screened in China.

Number of cinema screens in China from 2009 to 2019

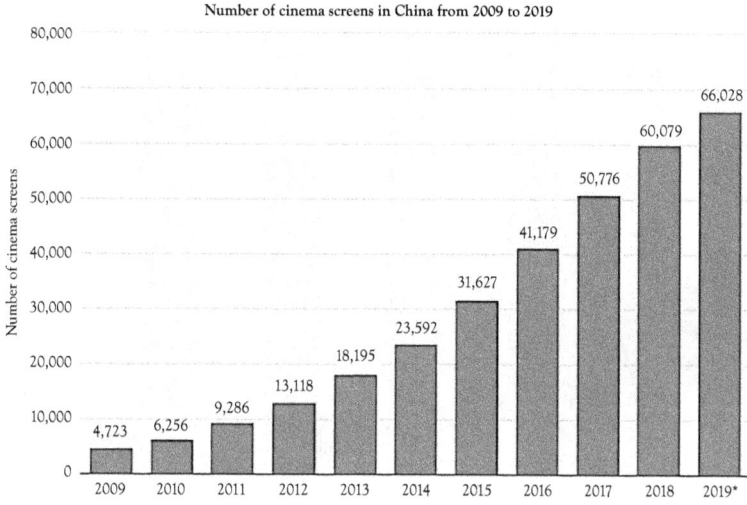

Number of cinema screens

Year	Screens
2009	4,723
2010	6,256
2011	9,286
2012	13,118
2013	18,195
2014	23,592
2015	31,627
2016	41,179
2017	50,776
2018	60,079
2019*	66,028

Opportunities by Region

China, far from being a single market, is a jigsaw puzzle of overlapping markets which are separated by demographics, dialects, culture, cuisine, and, of course, geography. One common temptation among first-timers is to pursue explosive growth focusing solely on geographic penetration rather than sustainability. This can produce impressive short-term results but exporters with limited means often find themselves quickly overextended and fighting copycat products and untrustworthy local distributors. It is always best to choose a region which suits your product and develop the brand at the local level, slowly but also sustainably.

The biggest opportunities in the food and beverage market can be found in the country's urban centers rather than in rural areas. About one-third of F&B companies are located in the eastern region, generating about 43 percent of the industrial value of that region. The major provinces in terms of F&B production are Shandong, Sichuan, Henan, Guangdong, Jiangsu, Liaoning, Hubei, Hunan, Fujian, and Jilin, which altogether account for around 66 percent of the total production value in this industry. Although there are more than 50,000 above-scale F&B industrial companies, 18 percent of the total value is a result of the 300 largest companies.

First-tier cities: First-tier cities such as Beijing, Shanghai, Shenzhen, Hangzhou, and increasingly Chengdu and Chongqing have experienced the greatest exposure to imported food and beverages. Multinational retail expansion has led to fierce competition in the wealthier coastal areas, but opportunities are still there.

Second- and third-tier cities: Incomes are rising rapidly in second- and third-tier cities, creating a new range of opportunities, while logistics and distribution still remain underdeveloped outside the largest urban centers, thus making distribution of imported products to interior cities hard.

The table indicates some of the available opportunities in China's urban centers by region:

Top 10 Provinces Based on F&B Production Value

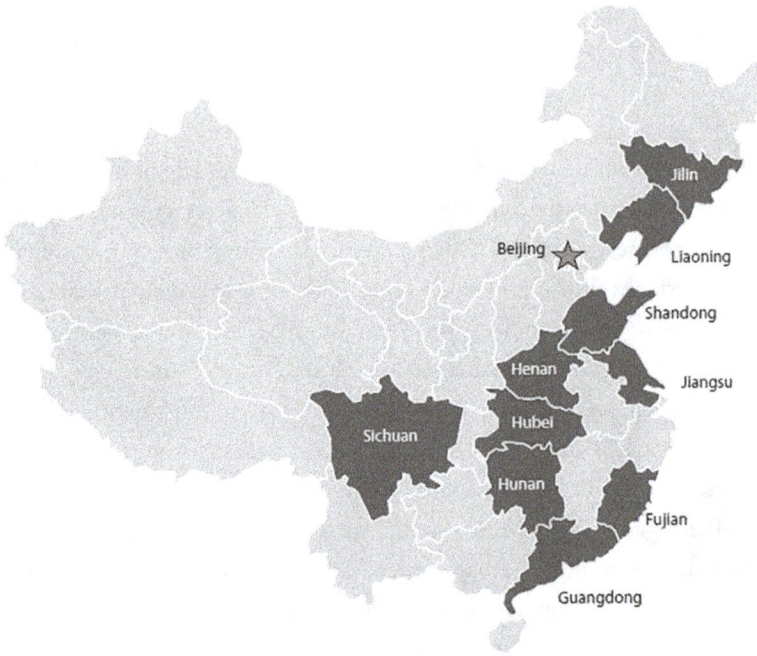

Source: JLI Ananlysis on multiple sources

Breakdown of China's total F&B production value

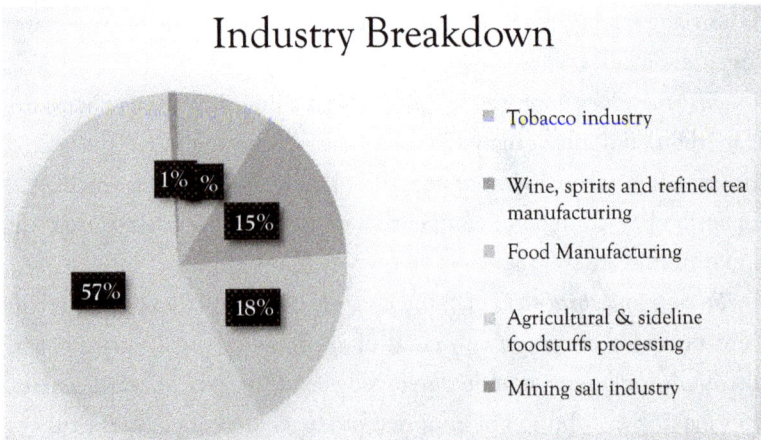

Source: EUSME Centre & USDA

	Food			Beverages	
	Chocolate, high-end confectionery, prepackaged biscuits and snacks	Dairy	Pasta, Pasta sauces and Olive Oil	Wine	Beer
Opportunities Across the Board	• Growing urban middle class. • Dining out at hotels, restaurants, cafes and bars is a huge growth area.. • Propensity for using western F&B products as gifts. • Continued market potential in first tier cities and growing markets in second and third tiers.				
Opportunities	• Demand growing as incomes increases. • Prepackaged snack foods and confectionery are popular for entertaining.	• Amongst the most popular imported products. • Food safety crises leading to preference for foreign products.	• has resonance with Chinese consumers.	• The largest EU export to china. • Potential in second and third tier cities.	• Opportunities for boutique beers. • Opportunities in second-tier cities.
Challenges Across the Board	• Cultural hurdles - On the whole, Chinese tastes and kitchens not yet ready for full adoption of western foods. • Increasing local competition. • Fragmented localised distribution channels. • Cold-chain storage under developed.				
Challenges	• Strong Japanese and Korean competition in snacks industry • US confectionery dominant at the upper and lower ends.	• Cold-chain distribution networks • Non-tariff barriers.	• Small profit margins require high volume sales.	• Countries wines flush the market. • Lack of consumer wine experience. • Mid-range quality wines are difficult to sell.	• Quality control, hygiene and distribution.
Legal Barriers	• Distribution of food is subject to the licensing system in China. Companies engaged in food distribution have to apply for the food distribution licence. • Manufacturers of certain imported food (for instance meat products) have to be registered with the Certification and Accreditation Administration (CNCA).			• Distribution of beverages is subject to the licensing system in China. Companies engaging in distribution of beverage have to apply for the food distribution licence. • Distributors of alcohol products must be filed with the local bureau of commerce.	
Taxes	• Corporation tax 25%. • VAT 17% / 13%. • City Maintenance and Construction Tax 1 - 7% of the VAT depending on location. • Education surcharge 3% of the VAT.				
Standard, Certification and Labelling requirements	• Sanitary certification is issued by the local quarantine bureau (CIQ) and based on products sample inspection. • Chinese national (GB) standards and professionals standards covering the technical quality and safety (hygiene) requirement, including food additives. • Labelling requirements for food, beverage and food for special dietary must be provided in chinese; lable must be verified by the local quarantine bureau.				

Market Barriers

Food and Beverage

Distribution

The food and beverage market remains decentralized in China, still lying in the condition of competition and free growth. There are very few large distributors dedicated to imported food and beverages. The varieties of products sold are also limited, as there are few importers or distributors with more than 1,000 varieties of imported food products. The great majority of Chinese distributors tend to be reluctant to introduce new products, are primarily interested in wholesaling, and do not put a lot of emphasis on brand development. They are mainly interested in products that are already present in the market but are sold through subdistributors or grey channels. Exporters with a limited product range need to work both ends of the supply chain simultaneously, trying to identify both retailers interested in the product and distributors who can work with the retailers.

Considering that imported food and beverages are typically higher priced compared to domestic equivalents, they are currently concentrated in first-tier cities in north, east, and south China, which has resulted in large distributors being based in these regions. As the economy grows, consumption in second- and third-tier cities is expected to increase fast, resulting in imported food and beverage products to transfer to these regions in the next years. At present, however, imported food and beverages in second- and third-tier cities are mainly supplied by importers and distributors from first-tier cities. With rising demand for imported food, the inefficient logistic channels of current distributors may encounter greater challenges and, as a result, the development of local distributors in second-tier cities will be of great importance to importers.

Infrastructure and Logistics

Shanghai, Beijing, and Guangzhou are the key entry points to China. Recent improvements in the national highway system have considerably eased trucking directly out of Shanghai or Guangzhou compared to a few years ago. High-speed rail has greatly reduced the travel time across the country and now trains from Shanghai to Hangzhou take half an hour and to Nanjing one hour. The Chinese government is continuing to support and develop the rail network. As for container ports, China has the largest ones in the world, with Shanghai holding the world's top spot since 2010. In the region of Guangzhou, Hong Kong and Shenzhen container ports come third and fourth, respectively, and China has another three ports within the world's largest 10.

Ports in satellite cities offer a growing array of services, often including bonded storage with temperature-controlled services, online tracking facilities, and duty-free industrial zones where goods can be repackaged or processed, with duty paid only on the original import value and only after the products have left the zone. However, further inland logistic services, inefficient and fragmented, make it difficult to transport products directly from the coast to inland cities. Importers are not very confident in cold chains.

Economies of Scale

Organic food producers, especially those with a geographical identification (GI) mark, face the challenge of scaling up their production capacity in order to meet local demand and produce at sufficient volume to make a profit. However, the quality of their products—and their GI status—depends on their small production capacity. On the other hand, China is a very large market, and if a product is successful, demand will grow beyond capacity. Considering the difficulties of entry and the costs involved, it can be a challenge to make a successful and profitable market entry.

Producing locally can make production and selling at quantity more affordable. For example, some Dutch and Hungarian companies have had some success by breeding geese locally and producing goose livers in partnership with Chinese producers. A Chinese company has established an Italian-style meat processing company which uses Italian processes and their products are marketed as Italian.

Increasing Local Competition

Western products are regarded as high quality and produced to high safety standards, but they tend to be pricier than their local equivalents. In terms of international competition, the United States remains the largest single exporter of consumer-oriented food to China. The country is the only exporter with a presence in most categories.

Local manufacturers tend to push imported products out of the price-sensitive mass market, into niche markets where novelty and quality are more important than price. In the past, bars and restaurants were often obliged to import all of their specialty Western products, but they are now able to turn to local producers. For instance, *Le Fromager de Pékin* sells cheese directly to hotels and restaurants and many local producers are now making European-style cured meats and other delicacies.

Exporting Goods

Process for Exporting Goods to China

The first step is always to determine what category the goods you want to export fall into. China's Ministry of Commerce (MOFCOM) regulates the imports of foreign goods. According to the New Foreign Trade Law, goods are classified into the following three categories, depending on how helpful they are for the Chinese' government's economic targets: free imports, restricted imports, and prohibited imports.

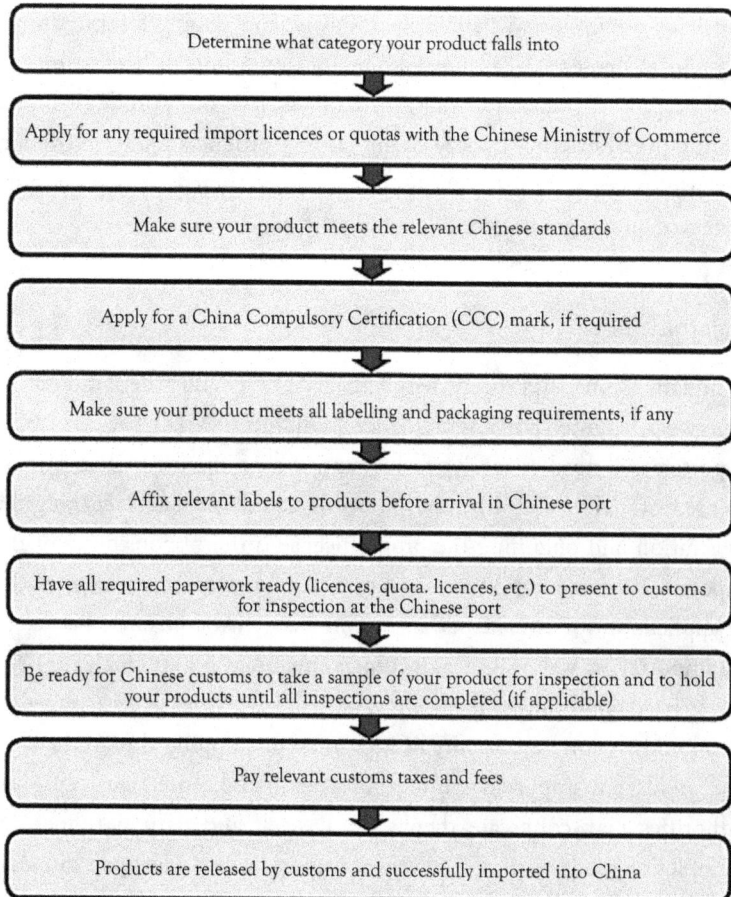

Determine what category your product falls into

⬇

Apply for any required import licences or quotas with the Chinese Ministry of Commerce

⬇

Make sure your product meets the relevant Chinese standards

⬇

Apply for a China Compulsory Certification (CCC) mark, if required

⬇

Make sure your product meets all labelling and packaging requirements, if any

⬇

Affix relevant labels to products before arrival in Chinese port

⬇

Have all required paperwork ready (licences, quota. licences, etc.) to present to customs for inspection at the Chinese port

⬇

Be ready for Chinese customs to take a sample of your product for inspection and to hold your products until all inspections are completed (if applicable)

⬇

Pay relevant customs taxes and fees

⬇

Products are released by customs and successfully imported into China

Process for Exporting Goods to China

Free Imports

Free importable goods are obviously the least regulated category of goods and can normally be imported into China without restriction. On the other hand, selected items do require an automatic import license which is granted to all companies who apply. This license enables the Chinese government to monitor the imported amounts of certain goods. The list of products that require this automatic license is jointly updated by MOFCOM and GAC (General Administration of Customs) on a regular basis.

Restricted Imports

Restricted are imports whereby the importer must apply for and obtain an import license, a tariff quota license, a quota import license, or any combination of these. According to Chinese law, only products under quantitative restriction by way of quotas and products under restriction by way of necessary licenses are considered as "restricted." Products under tariff-rate quotas are not considered "restricted."

Import License

Although China has been reducing red tape and the amount of paperwork required for imports since joining the WTO back in 2001, importers still need to receive formal approval in the form of an import license from MOFCOM before importing certain products. Making the registration and obtaining the proper license is the responsibility of the importer. Documentation required to obtain an import license includes an application for issuance of an import license, the business license of the importer, as well as other documents required for specific categories of restricted goods under the license system. It is crucial to verify whether your goods require an import license prior to shipping the product. In case goods are imported without the required license, local customs authorities may confiscate them. Wool, steel, and natural rubber are examples of goods restricted by way of import license. Next you can see a sample list of goods subject to automatic import license:

Goods subject to automatic import licence (for reference only)		
Poultry	Crude oil	Vegetable oil
Processed oil	Waster paper	Alumina
Tobacco	Chemical fertilizer	Cellulose diacetate filament tow
Copper ore and concentrates	Copper	Coal
Aluminium	Mechanic and electrical products	Iron ore
Steel		

Goods subject to import licence (for reference only)	
Specific used chemical and electrical products	Ozone-depleting substances

MOFCOM's official catalogues for goods subject to automatic import license can be found online (in Chinese). Lists are updated on a regular basis.

Import Quotas

An import quota is the maximum amount of foreign goods that can be imported into a country in a given period of time. It is, in fact, a type of trade restriction used to limit the supply of foreign goods available in the market, which results in a higher market price of these goods. Certain goods are regulated under a quota management, meaning that China will allow only a certain quantity of these goods to enter the borders each year. In this case, importers have to apply for a relevant import quota license prior to importing any goods into China. Examples of such products are pesticides, tobacco, and crude oil.

Tariff-Rate Quota Management

An import license is also required in order to import goods under tariff-rate quota management. Goods under tariff-rate quota management, among others, include grain, cotton, sugar, and vegetable oil.

Next you can see a sample list of goods subject to tariff-rate quota management:

Goods under tariff-rate quota management (for reference only)		
Grain	Chemical fertilizer	Vegetable oil
Cotton	Sugar	

Prohibited Imports

Certain goods are prohibited from import into China for health, environmental, and national security reasons. It is unlikely that your goods will be on this list. Prohibited goods include illicit drugs, weapons, ammunition, or explosives. Next you can see a sample list of goods prohibited from import:

Prohibited imports (for reference only)		
Arms	Lethal poisons	Old/used garments
Ammunition	Illicit Drugs	Explosives
Disease-carrying animals and plants	Food items containing certain food coloring and additives deemed harmful to human health	Printed matter; magnetic media, films or photographs which are deemed detrimental to the political, economic, cultural, and moral interests of China
Foods, medicine and other articles coming from disease-stricken areas		

Standards

Once you have checked and confirmed the import category your goods fall into and once you have gathered the necessary documentation, you will need to ensure that your products meet the corresponding Chinese standards. *Although some Chinese standards might correlate with international standards, it does not mean that you will automatically meet the Chinese standards.*

There are four levels of standards in China: national standards, professional standards, local standards, and enterprise standards. Be aware that it is only national standards or Guobiao (GB) standards that are mandatory. The others are considered voluntary. Standard levels are also hierarchical; meeting the highest existing standard for your product means that you automatically meet all lower-level standards.

However, certain product categories may require compliance with professional and national standards, since those standards usually regulate different aspects of the product. Never launch big initiatives with only the support of the local government and not the central one. The central government's plans will ultimately prevail, no matter how many connections local interests may have. The business landscape is littered with ventures that failed because companies failed to gain support from enough layers of the government.

Authorities

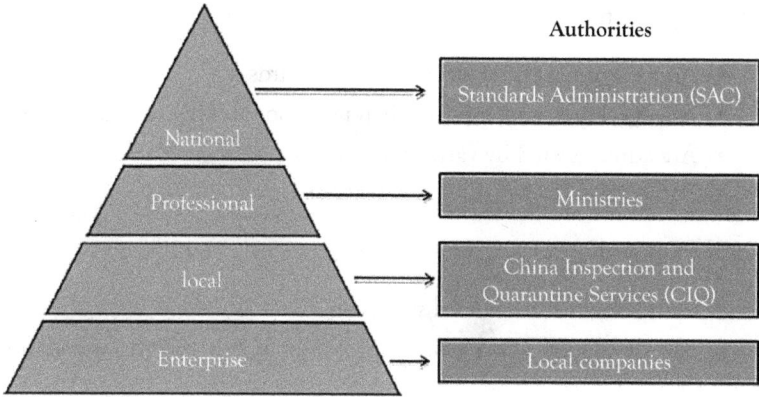

National → Standards Administration (SAC)

Professional → Ministries

Local → China Inspection and Quarantine Services (CIQ)

Enterprise → Local companies

National Standards

Administered nationally by the Standardization Administration of China (SAC) and consistent across China, 15 percent of national (GB) standards are mandatory. The SAC has a database of over 27,000 national standards.

Next you can see an online National Standard Query Form which you can use to get more information based on the specifics of the products you want to import:

Professional Standards

- Also known as sector or industry standards
- Are developed and applied when no national (GB) standards apply
- Are administered by various ministries

Local Standards

- Also known as provincial standards
- Are developed when neither professional nor national standards apply
- Administered by China Inspection and Quarantine Service (CIQ)
- Designated with either "DB+*" (mandatory) or "DB+*/T" (voluntary)

Enterprise Standards

- Developed and used by companies when higher-level standards are not available
- Never mandatory

Standards prefix GB followed by the standards code

Code	Content
GB	Mandatory national standards
GB/T	Voluntary national standards
GB/Z	National guiding technical document

Source: SAC

Industry Sector Standards

Code	Content	Code	Content	Code	Content
BB	Packaging	JG	Construction industry	SN	Commodity
CB	Ship	JR	Finance	SY	Petroleum gas
CH	Surveying	UT	Communication	SY (>10000)	Oceanic petroleum gas
CJ	Urban construction	UY	Education	TB	Railways transportation
CY	Press and publication	LB	Tourism	TD	land administration
DA	Archives	LD	Labour and labour safety	TY	Sport
DB	Earthquake	LY	Forestry	WB	Goods
DL	Power	MH	Civil avaiation	WH	Culture
DZ	Geology mineral	MT	Coal	WJ	Civil products from arms industry
EJ	Nuclear industry	MZ	Civil affairs	WM	Foreign trade
FZ	Textiles	NY	Agriculture	WS	Hygiene
GA	Public security	QB	Light industry	XB	Rare earth
GY	Radio, film & TV	QC	Automobiles	YB	Ferrous metallurgy
HB	Aviation	QJ	Space	YC	Tobacco
HG	Chemical industry	QX	Meterology	YD	Telecommunication
HJ	Environmental protection	SB	Commmerce	YS	Non-ferrous metallurgy
HS	Customs	SC	Water product	YY	Medicine
HY	Ocean	SH	Petro-chemical industry	YZ	Postal
JB	Machinery	SJ	Electronics		
JC	Building materials	SL	Water resources		

Source: SAC

China Compulsory Certification

The China Compulsory Certification (CCC) mark is China's national safety and quality mark. It is administered by the Certification and Accreditation Administration and the China Certification Center. It is compulsory and must be obtained before your products can be imported and sold in China. This CCC mark takes the form of a physical sticker that is applied to individual products as a label. It is required for approximately 20 percent of EU exports to China. The CNCA publishes an online catalogue of CCC mandatory products, grouped into 23 categories and spanning 254 products. Because CQC and CNCA periodically make amendments to this list, it is important that you use the most recent version when checking whether your product is listed. CCC mandatory products, among others, include household and small electrical appliances, latex products, motor vehicles, medical devices, and high-tech products.

In case the CCC certification is required, it is highly recommended to work with an experienced local third-party consultant, partner, or contractor to obtain the approval. This helps a lot with language, culture, and distance barriers, thus significantly speeding up the process. While relatively cumbersome, the certification process is pretty straightforward and can be completed within four to six months. Costs start at 3,500 euros and can range upwards significantly, always depending on the specifics of each product. Once CCC certification is obtained, it will be valid for five years but must be renewed on an annual basis. The unauthorized supply, import, or sale of products listed in the CCC catalogue may result in product confiscation at the border or in a penalty fee ranging from 8,000 to 50,000 RMB or more.

CCC Mark Certification Process

The CCC mark certification involves six main steps:

- *Application*: Submission of application and supporting materials to CNCA.
- *Testing*: Submission of product to CQC laboratory in China for testing.
- *Factory inspection*: Inspection of factory and manufacturing facilities by CQC.
- *Evaluation*: Approval of CCC certificate or failure and retesting.
- *Product marking*: Marking and packaging of the product with the approved CCC mark.

- *Annual follow-up factory inspections*: Manufacturing facilities need to be inspected every 12 to 18 months. Follow-up inspection costs are much lower than the initial inspection.

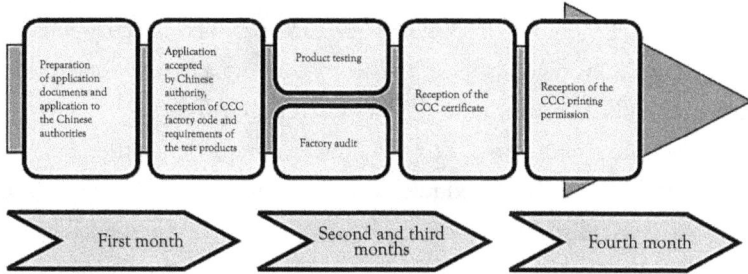

Other Industry Standards

In addition to GB standards and the CCC mark, many government agencies in China are able to issue industry-specific standards or testing requirements for products under their jurisdiction. For instance, the export of food, medical devices, and cosmetics must also receive approval by State Food & Drug Administration (SFDA) before import into China. It is necessary to refer to specific industry guidelines for your particular product.

Packaging

In addition to standards and labeling, there is a number of packaging requirements for all goods exported to China. Depending on the specific product, packaging requirements can vary greatly because they are administered by different government bodies. For packaging laws and standards, you may check the packaging regulations of your specific industry.

Commodity Inspection and Customs

The AQSIQ (General Administration for Quality Supervision, Inspection & Quarantine) is the main administrative and enforcement body for quality control, measurement, entry–exit health quarantine, inspection of import and export commodities, and certification and standardization in China. The Catalogue of Import-Export Commodities Subject to Compulsory Inspection & Quarantine is the official document listing the types of commodities that require entry–exit inspection and quarantine and explaining how the inspections for each product category will be carried out. Once goods pass the entry–exit commodity inspection process, an official certificate will be awarded from AQSIQ.

Once your goods arrive at the Chinese port or any other port of entry to China, they will need to clear customs inspection. Your Chinese importer (your distributor or your local agent) will be responsible for gathering all necessary documents and provide them to the Chinese customs agent. Note that the approval process for these documents should begin long in advance of your product's arrival in China, in order to ensure smooth passage through customs.

Although required customs documentation varies from one product to another, standard procedures include:

- Import license inspection (if applied)/quota certificate
- Customs registration
- Commodity inspection
- Customs declaration
- Submission of various documents (certificates of origin, bills of landing, sales contracts, packing lists, commercial invoices, etc.)
- Examination
- Payment of taxes and fees

Taxes and Fees for the Import of Goods

Many taxes and fees are associated with the export of goods to China. The most common ones are listed here:

- For customs duty purposes, the taxable value of an imported good is its cost, insurance, and freight price, which includes the normal transaction price of the goods, plus the cost of freight, insurance, packing, and seller's commission.

- Chinese customs are in charge of assessing the customs duty of all imports.
- Customs use a valuation database listing the values of various imports based on international as well as domestic market prices.
- Customs officers will typically accept the importer's price but if the imported value is too far out of line with the database, customs officers will most likely estimate the value of goods based on national custom rules and regulations for tax calculation purposes.

To look up tariff rates, please search for your product by HS code at the China Customs website.

Value-Added Taxes

- Value-added tax (VAT) is levied on the sales and import of goods as well as processing, replacement, and repair services.
- VAT is levied after the tariff and incorporates the value of the tariff.
- VAT is collected on imports at the point of entry into China.
- The basic VAT rate is currently 17 percent but a lower rate of 13 percent applies to the following product categories (among others): drinking water, food and edible vegetable oil, heating, liquefied petroleum gas, coal gas, natural gas, books, magazines, newspapers, animal feed, pesticides, chemical fertilizers, agricultural plastic sheeting, and agricultural machinery.
- Importers may enjoy tax exemption for the import of certain goods identified in relevant regulations. For instance, the import of devices for the use in teaching and scientific research might be exempted.

Consumption Tax

- Fourteen categories of goods are subject to consumption tax, which can be calculated based on the price and amount of the imported goods respectively or collectively, depending on the specific legal regulations.

- The rate of the consumption tax is calculated based on the price of the goods and is between 1 and 5 percent.
- Goods subject to consumption tax include liquor, tobacco, cosmetics, precious jewelry, precious jade and stones, refined oil products, firecrackers and fireworks, motorcycles, motor vehicle tires, small motor vehicles, yachts, golfing equipment, high-grade watches, real wood flooring, and wooden chopsticks.

Exporting Services

Since joining the WTO, China has gradually opened up its service industry to foreign businesses, especially the securities, insurance and banking, logistics, and telecommunications sectors. Services in these sectors are urgently needed in China due to the country's rapid economic growth, requiring high expertise, large investments, and advanced technology. As Western companies often offer stronger services in these industries than their Chinese counterparts, China's service imports have grown rapidly in the last couple of years. In 2020, China became the largest importer of services worldwide, while yearly trade in services has seen an annual growth rate of about 11 percent.

According to the General Agreement on Trade in Services under the WTO framework, trade in services, which is also known as import of services, is defined as the supply of a given service:

- From the territory of one member state into the territory of another member state
- In the territory of one member state to the service consumer of any other member state
- By a service supplier of one member state through commercial presence in the territory of any other member state
- By a service supplier of one member state, through presence of natural persons of a member state in the territory of any other member state

Process for Exporting Services to China

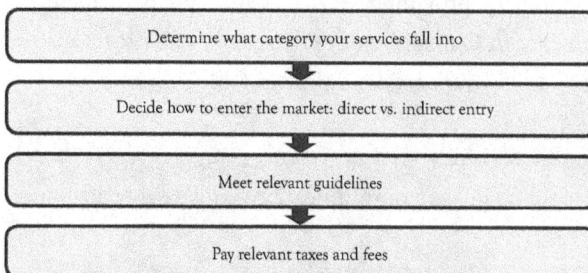

Determine what category your services fall into
Decide how to enter the market: direct vs. indirect entry
Meet relevant guidelines
Pay relevant taxes and fees

For the sake of clarity, exports of services to China are divided into direct market entry covering investment and indirect market entry covering the rest.

Direct Market Entry

– : requires more resources

+: provides full market access

Open an office on the ground in China by establishing a foreign-invested enterprise and provide services as you normally would in other places where you have an office. FIEs are subject to all laws, taxes, and regulations as laid forth by the Chinese government. For more information on FIEs and options for which type to establish, please refer to my book *Entering the Chinese Market*.

Indirect Market Entry

– : provides only limited market access

+: requires fewer resources

Export your products to China without setting up an office on the ground.

Once an agreement is reached with the Chinese client, you can send a representative or a consultant to China on a short-term basis if it is necessary.

It works best if you are looking to build a customer base in China for services that you provide in your home country, for example, travel services.

It does not work well for services that you would like to provide on the ground in China, mainly because Chinese business culture values personal interactions and face-to-face meetings.

One option for providing services without a permanent or on-the-ground presence in China is to offer them online. Basic resources required to market and sell your services online in China include:

- Chinese website
- Chinese language communication skills (either in-house or contracted)

- Flexibility to take calls and virtual meetings during China working hours
- Ability to send employees on a short-term basis to China
- Ability to accept international payments via wire transfer or credit card

Services Allowed for Investment

A big number of services are approved for provision in China. In the 13th Five-Year Plan, MOFCOM released a blueprint for the development of the service trade industry. The plan, jointly drafted by MOFCOM and 33 other ministries and organizations, calls for further development of services in 30 sectors, including transportation, tourism, construction, finance, and technology. Since 2010, education-related travel services have been representing the largest foreign service export to China.

Service Sectors Encouraged and Permitted for Investment

Permitted services are all services which are not included in the Investment Catalogue and those not falling in a "special regulations" category. Government approval for investment in the "encouraged" and "permitted" categories is normally granted automatically. Encouraged industries generally bring innovation or advanced technology to China, increase efficiency and product quality, or protect the environment and conserve resources.

Service activities in industries such as education, transportation, manufacturing, art, culture, film, radio, and television fall in the "permitted and encouraged" category.

Service Sectors Restricted for Investment

Investments in restricted industries face stricter scrutiny from the Chinese government and demand higher levels of approval. Certain sectors might be classified as restricted for a number of reasons, including when China does not stand to gain innovative technology, if the industry has an adverse effect on the environment, or if for any other reason, the industry is highly regulated by the State Council. Although it is not impossible, services in restricted sectors are much harder to export to China. As a way of entering such sectors, China may require foreign companies to establish a joint venture with a local partner. Some service activities in sectors such as real estate and high-end property, banking and insurance, telecommunications, and medical institutions are restricted.

Service Sectors Prohibited for Investment

Services falling in the "prohibited" sectors category are completely off-limits to foreign investors. These industries are prohibited because the Chinese government has deemed that their import might harm public health, the environment, or national security or lead to loss of Chinese intellectual property. Prohibited service sectors include social research, postal services, and the publication of books, newspapers, and magazines.

Taxes and Fees for the Import of Services

Based on current Chinese laws and regulations, all service companies that have earned income in China or have consumers located in China are subject to Chinese taxes, unless exempted expressly by Chinese regulations. Such taxes vary depending on the industry, income, location of service, and business model.

Direct Market Entry and Establishment of an FIE to Provide Services

Subject to all taxes applicable to a foreign invested enterprise:
Business tax: usually 3 to 5 percent
Enterprise income tax: 25 percent (rate for SMEs under Chinese law is 20 percent)
Individual income tax: 3 to 45 percent
VAT pilot tax: 3, 6, 11, or 17 percent
Other applicable taxes and fees as regulated by Chinese government ministries, depending on locality and industry.

Indirect Market Entry, No Office on the Ground

Unless exempted expressly by Chinese laws and regulations, foreign service providers are subject to a business tax, which is normally 3 to 5 percent for the income derived from provision of services to Chinese service receivers, as well as surtaxes like maintenance and city construction tax, and education surcharge.

For the sake of reference, next you can see a more specific sector business tax table:

Taxable Item	Business Tax Rate
Communications and transportation, construction, telecommunications and post	3%
Finance, investment and Insurance, transfer or intangible assets, transfer of immovable property	5%
Entertainment	5%–20%

Reform of Service Industry Taxation

Since 2012, a pilot reform regarding the collection of VAT in lieu of a business tax (BT) in the transportation and parts of modern service industries has been progressively implemented in China. Where international service providers provide such services to Chinese entities or individuals, they are subject to VAT for the income derived from the services instead of business tax, as long as a number of conditions are met.

Tax Treaties

Foreign service providers are subject to enterprise income tax at the rate of 10 percent of the deemed taxable income, calculated based on the income derived from selling the service. On the other hand, the enterprise income tax that a foreign service provider is required to pay may be mitigated by tax treaties. These tax treaties signed between countries are aimed at reducing double taxation, eliminating tax evasion, and encouraging cross-border trade efficiency.

Exporting Technology

Technology transfer is the process of transferring patent rights, rights to apply for patents, licenses for the exploitation of patents, technological know-how, technical secrets, as well as the provision of technical services and technology transfers in other forms. Access to growing Chinese demand for high-tech products and services, establishment of R&D facilities, access to a large number of suppliers and an increasingly skilled work force, engagement in cooperative development, and the establishment of long-term partnerships with Chinese businesses are only a few of the reasons guiding Western investors' decision to export and sell their technology to China.

One way to get a foothold in China is to license or transfer ownership of your key technology and designs to Chinese subsidiaries of Western firms, joint venture partners, or Chinese manufacturing and service companies. One of the major challenges facing Western companies using this way to enter the Chinese market is devising creative solutions to minimize risks to their intellectual property rights resulting from such technology transfers.

Process of Transferring Technology to China

Technology transfers are not limited to high technology. Many companies manufacture low-technology, consumer and industrial products and designs in China through a manufacturing contract. No matter the level of technology, all foreign companies transferring technology to China face the same IP rights.

```
┌─────────────────────────────────────────────────────────────┐
│   Make sure your technology is registered and protected       │
│              in your home market                              │
└─────────────────────────────────────────────────────────────┘
                          ▼
┌─────────────────────────────────────────────────────────────┐
│           Register and protect your technology in China       │
└─────────────────────────────────────────────────────────────┘
                          ▼
┌─────────────────────────────────────────────────────────────┐
│         Find out what category your technology falls into     │
└─────────────────────────────────────────────────────────────┘
                          ▼
┌─────────────────────────────────────────────────────────────┐
│        Decide between licensing and ownership transfer        │
└─────────────────────────────────────────────────────────────┘
                          ▼
┌─────────────────────────────────────────────────────────────┐
│                   Find a Chinese partner                      │
└─────────────────────────────────────────────────────────────┘
                          ▼
┌─────────────────────────────────────────────────────────────┐
│           Negotiate a technology transfer contract            │
└─────────────────────────────────────────────────────────────┘
```

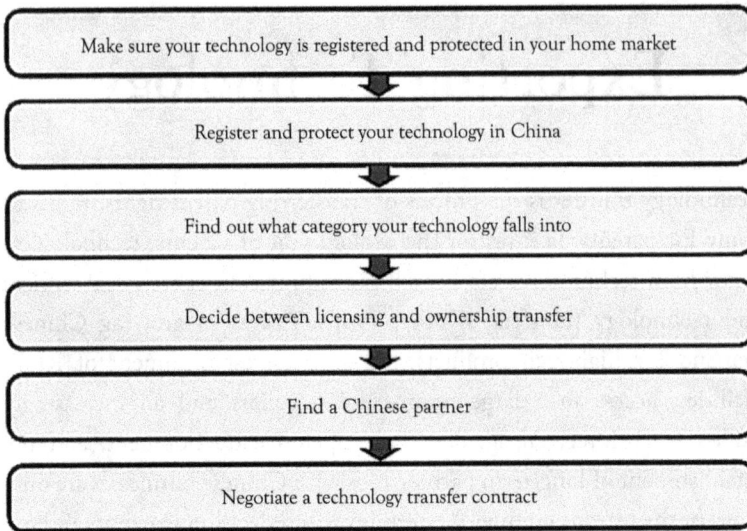

What Is Patent Licensing?

Based on the exclusive rights conferred by a patent, licensing is a permission granted by the patent owner to another party to use the patented invention on agreed terms and conditions (including, for instance, the payment of royalties), while the patent owner continues to retain ownership of the patent. Licensing not only creates a source of income for the patent owner but also establishes a legal framework for the transfer of that technology.

Methods of Transferring Technology

Licensing

Common practice. It includes know-how, patents, designs, and technical secrets.

Ownership Transfer

This is an uncommon practice. Generally not recommended due to intellectual property risks. There are three main ways of exporting your technology to China.

Licensing the Technology to an Unrelated Chinese Company

When licensing to unrelated Chinese companies, you generally have the least control over your IP. A "modular strategy" can be used, one which involves different Chinese suppliers to source different components of your product, so that no single Chinese supplier will be able to duplicate your technology. You can also use a phased implementation of your licensing contract to test out your Chinese partner before transferring additional technology. Both strategies are widely used by many Western companies.

Setting Up a Joint Venture

In certain industries, Chinese law requires foreign businesses to establish a joint venture in order to transfer technology to a Chinese partner. Make sure you check the Foreign Investment Catalogue published by the National Development and Reform Commission to see if your company will be required to do this. Apart from the Investment Catalogue, the requirement to set up a joint venture can result from other legislation and regulations as well.

Although it will be hard to use a modular approach with your Chinese JV partner, it is still essential that you take steps to protect your IP. Many foreign companies keep critical design and IP components overseas or held in a wholly separate WOFE. A Chinese JV partner's local contacts and distribution network are valuable in a distribution and sales role.

Setting Up a WOFE

If a WOFE is permitted in your industry, it will give you the greatest amount of control over your IR rights. In this type of entity, IP risk should be managed by preventing leaks by employees and business partners, while the use of incomplete confidentiality agreements is equally important.

Technology Approved for Import

In China, it is MOFCOM that regulates the import of technology. Technology imports are divided into three main groups:

- Freely importable
- Restricted
- Prohibited

The Ministry of Commerce publishes lists of technologies prohibited or restricted for import and updates them regularly. Technology not included in the restricted or prohibited category is freely importable. Apart from a few sectors deemed harmful to national interests or national security, most technology falls within the freely importable category. This type of technology can be imported directly without prior approval, although the importer must register the technology transfer contract with MOFCOM.

Registration can be started online but will have to be finished on-site at MOFCOM. Since a registration certificate is needed to be able to carry out foreign exchange, banking, tax, customs, and other transfer-related issues, it is highly recommended as a practical matter.

Restricted Technology

There are currently around 100 technology categories that are restricted for import. The rationale for restricting this type of technology is as follows:

- They are likely to endanger national security.
- They are likely to be harmful to the health of human beings, animals, and plants.
- They are likely to damage the environment.
- They are likely to have a negative impact on public interests and public moral.

A listing on the restricted catalogue does not make the technology impossible to import; it just makes it harder. In order to import from this list of restricted technology, an import license must first be obtained from MOFCOM. A contract for the import of restricted technology is only legally effective after an import license is obtained.

Applications for restricted technology-related licenses must be submitted to the competent branch of MOFCOM at provincial level. Once the application is submitted, MOFCOM will review the trade and technical aspects. They are required to make a decision within 30 working days on whether or not to approve the application.

Factors considered by MOFCOM when reviewing applications for import licenses include whether the import:

- Complies with China's foreign trade policies and external trade obligations.
- Promotes the development of foreign economic cooperation.
- Endangers national security or threatens the public interest.
- Endangers lives and the health of people.
- Damages the country's ecological system.
- Complies with state industrial policies and economic development strategies, accelerates technological progress, and supports the country's economic and technological rights and interests. In case the application is approved, MOFCOM has 10 working days to review the authenticity of the import contract before reaching a final decision on whether to issue an import license. In addition, once the import license is granted, the importer is required to complete an online registration of the contract.

Updates must be registered with MOFCOM for approval if:

- Substantial modifications to the contract require an application for a new import license.
- A contract is terminated.

Prohibited Technology

There are 10 categories of technology prohibited from import into China that are currently listed in the MOFCOM's import catalogue. These include technologies related to chemical engineering, nonferrous metal processing, and petrochemical production.

Technology Transfer Contract

In order to transfer your technology into China, you will need to enter into a technology transfer agreement with a Chinese partner. Technology transfer contracts are those involving the import of technology and include contracts for:

- Transfer of patent rights
- Transfer of the right to apply for the patent
- Transfer of technological know-how
- License for the exploitation of patents

All of these need to be in written form.

Process and Content for a Technology Transfer Contract

1. *File for intellectual property rights protection.*
   Make sure you have filed for the appropriate IPR protection of the technology you want to import (trademark, patent, copyright, etc.) both within your home country and in China before entering into any technology transfer negotiation.
2. *Confirm technology is legally importable in China.*
   Consult MOFCOM's catalogues of restricted and prohibited technology to see if your technology is freely importable into China. In case it falls into the restricted technology category, make sure you have applied for and received an import license from the relevant government bodies.
3. *Choose a reliable Chinese partner.*
   Conduct due diligence and carry out a thorough check of your potential local partners, as well as local industrial policies and laws. It is paramount to be aware that a major motivation for most Chinese companies in a technology transfer is to obtain foreign know-how through the technology they import. This is an industry fact and choosing the right Chinese partner is crucial as a first step to protecting your intellectual property in a technology transfer. Keep in mind that the ideal partner should be complimentary and not well positioned to directly compete with your business.

4. *Negotiate a technology transfer agreement.*

The structure of your technology transfer contract is critical as your whole IP protection will depend on it. It is recommended that you use IP licenses with your prospective Chinese partners. In addition to establishing each party's rights, the IP license ensures that the technology being transferred is documented, in case issues arise later on.

The contract should define clearly and document the technology in question, establish each party's rights, and include specific clauses for improvement and confidentiality. Important points that should be included in a technology transfer contract include the following:

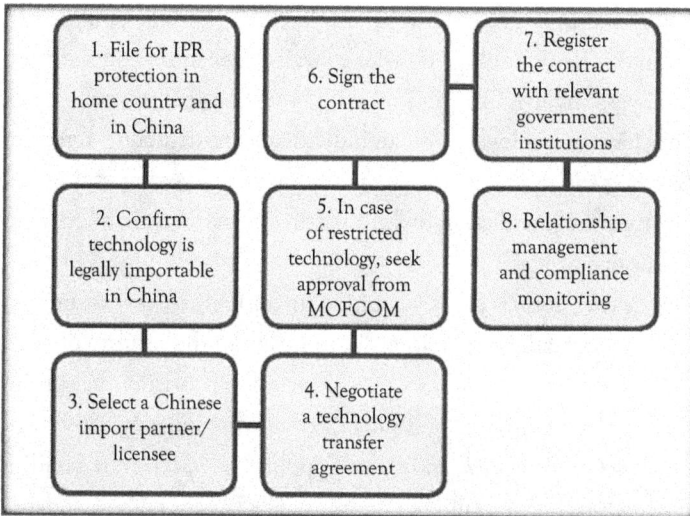

Clearly define in writing with your partner the specific technology in question as well as the rights each party has. The recipient of the transfer should be defined in detail as well as who may use the technology and how. When possible, license technology to Chinese partners instead of transferring ownership rights. It is important to make sure that the sharing of technology and information through documents, oral communications, and drawings must be clearly recorded and covered by the contract.

One of the most negotiated clauses of a technology transfer agreement is the creation of improvements and the ownership of improvements made by the Chinese partner. Unless specified by the agreement, commissioned IP belongs to the commissioned party, which means that if your Chinese partner develops improvements on top of your technology, they will own the IP rights to those improvements and, in practice, they will be able to copy and use your transferred technology freely. Be aware that, under Chinese law, a Chinese partner is allowed to make improvements and adjustments to transferred technology and use them. For these reasons it can be very risky to transfer or license your technology to a Chinese partner. Special attention needs to be paid to the improvement clause when preparing your technology transfer contract to provide legal protection to your IP.

Confidentiality. It is crucial to include strong confidentiality provisions in the technology transfer contract. Depending on the amount of employees involved in the process of the transfer, you may want to consider having employees sign an individual confidentiality agreement.

Noncompetition agreements. To avoid unnecessary competition, make sure to limit the jurisdiction of your partner to markets that you are currently not operating in.

Reverse engineering. RE is permitted under Chinese law and not considered theft of trade secrets. In order to maintain the security of your IP, the technology transfer contract should include a provision that prohibits your Chinese partner from engaging in reverse engineering activities.

Personnel and technical training. If applicable, specify the conditions under which technical training of employees will occur.

Limitations. Specify that the Chinese part cannot sell the technology to third parties without authorization. In addition, try to limit the amount of sublicenses given to them.

Price, payment, and taxes. Specify the value of the contract, how payments will be made, and who will be responsible for taxes in each market.

Delivery terms and packaging. Specify how the technology will be packaged and delivered to your Chinese partner as well as a timeline for delivery.

Termination. Include a clause for the termination of the contract beforehand and a timeline for the end of the contract. The agreement can always be amended and modified in the future. In case of restricted technology, seek approval from relevant MOFCOM branch.

Sign the contract. The contract is only valid if signed by both parties. In case of restricted technology, the agreement only becomes effective when the technology import license is issued.

Register the contract. The contract must be registered with the competent branch of MOFCOM within 60 days of its signing or within 60 days after the initial base amount of commission can be claimed in case the payment is made on a commission basis.

Management and compliance. Stay in regular communication with your partner to ensure compliance and maintain the partnership. Successful agreements are managed by both sides. Good contract management will ensure sound and profitable collaboration.

Taxes and Fees for the Transfer of Technology

There are certain fees and taxes owed by both parties that ente0r into a technology transfer agreement.

Chinese party: For any transfer or license of intellectual property, the Chinese party must register their tax obligation with the relevant Chinese tax bureau within 30 days of signing the contract. In addition to all other required documentation, they must present the signed contract to the tax authorities as it is only after registration that the Chinese party can pay taxes on behalf of the foreign party. In case the contract is a license, the Chinese party must file for taxes before each payment on behalf of the foreign party. Tax registration is essential if a contract includes payment of more than U.S. $30,000 (approximately) as it is not possible for a foreign party to receive such payments without a tax certificate.

Foreign party: Based on Chinese tax law, if the foreign party does not have an establishment in China, technology transfers are normally taxed at a rate of 20 percent on the gross sales price. In certain cases, with the right authority approvals, income may be taxed at 10 percent or less, or even fully exempt.

Distribution Channels

Import and distribution channels are complex and do change frequently. Import procedures must be handled by licensed importers who often also function as distributors. However, be aware that the great majority of the food distributors and traders are rather unlikely to hold import licenses. In fact, Hong Kong traders offer the least risk when acting as importers and distributors because they can arrange payments in foreign currencies and possess a wide distribution network. On the other hand, Chinese traders are usually reluctant to open lines of credit and often lack a deep understanding of international trading practices. MOFCOM, the Chinese Ministry of Commerce, maintains a searchable platform of importers, called the World Importer Net. Although it is inexhaustive, their website divides F&B importers into nine large and a few more specific categories based on the HS code of each importer's food and beverages. This allows users to search in specific categories in a given geographical area. For instance, in the category HS CODE 220300 (Beverages, Spirits and Vinegar), there are currently 19 importers in Shanghai and 12 importers in Beijing. In addition, users can find listed the country of origin of the imports and the major import products for each importer.

In China, there is a contradiction between the underlying retail distribution network—which remains localized and fragmented—and the affluent appearance of many local shopping precincts. This can impact the success of both retailers and importers. There is no nationwide network of highways, trucks, and cold storage warehouses to efficiently deliver supplies from the importer or the manufacturer to the store shelf.

The major foreign retailers, including Tesco and Carrefour, are attempting every possible effort to build up a high-efficiency distribution network through a central distribution center. The problem is that they have no large regional distribution centers and the infrastructure of the current centers cannot meet the demand to deliver efficiently supplies from the importer or manufacturer to the store shelves. Generally, distribution is handled on a city-by-city or a store-by-store basis, with stores receiving most imports from various local distributors which increase the costs.

Available distribution channels

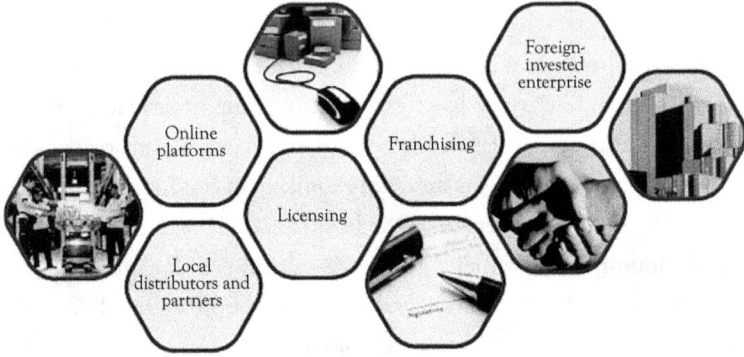

Adapted from USDA China Retail Report 2017

Import Requirements

The table here provides a detailed introduction to the steps that are required to import prepackaged food in China. This information is as accurate as possible but it may not be complete as procedures and timeframes vary depending on local regulations and specific good categories. Exemptions from food import procedures are allowed for the diplomatic community (embassies, consulates, and duty-free stores), food for use at exhibitions and fairs, as well as sample food. Small quantities of food stuffs imported for sampling or trial sales are not exempted and must go through standard inspection and certification procedures. Your distributor, importer, or agent should take the exemption from Chinese labeling procedures to the appropriate local food inspection agency before the goods arrive in China.

Labeling

All foreign products entering China require a certain amount of labeling, normally in Chinese. Labels are administered by China Inspection and Quarantine (CIQ). It is always best to get approval from CIQ, receive the labels, and attach them to the products before they arrive in the Chinese port. For first-time exporters the whole process of labeling and customs clearance can be quite an ordeal. However, being consistent and using the same port as point of entry into China will make the process much easier with time. For detailed information on labeling requirements you can visit the website of the General Administration of Quality Supervision, Inspection and Quarantine of the People's Republic of China.

Labeling requirements often change. Exporters are advised to reconfirm requirements for labeling and other certifications prior to dispatching their goods for export. While similar measures and procedures are employed by other importing countries, China's requirements are generally greater than those of other importing countries. China applies import regulations, which can have an adverse effect on trade due to increased costs and compliance difficulties.

The cost of obtaining a Chinese label can vary significantly. Customs charges are generally calculated as a percentage of the value of the imported products. Fees include label verification, product inspection, and quarantine. There are two types of labeling in China.

Mandatory Labeling

For certain product categories both Chinese and English labels are required. Labeling requirements vary by industry and subsector.

Food and Beverage

Labels must contain information on weight and volume, the ingredients, composition of each ingredient, as well as the address of the manufacturer and local distributor.

Label approval applications are normally submitted in advance of the first shipment of goods and determined together with the first sampling and inspection process.

The label should include, inter alia:

- Name and trademark of the product
- The manufacturer's name and address
- Date of manufacture
- Type of food
- Country of origin
- Net weight and volume
- Ingredients in descending volume by weight or volume
- Expiry date
- Usage instructions
- Batch number
- Standard code

Label Requirements: Food for Special Dietary Uses

All imported prepackaged foods for special dietary uses must be labeled in both English and Chinese (simplified) with the General Standard for the Labeling of Prepackaged Foods for Special Dietary Uses. The following is the minimum required information to be listed:

- Food name
- List of ingredients and exact weight or volume of each ingredient
- Nutrient
- Net weight or volume
- Name and address of manufacture of local distributor or agent
- Production date and guidance for storing
- Edible method, recommended intake, and targeted people
- Code of national, industrial, or enterprise standard for the product
- Quality grade

The labeling of prepackaged food for special dietary uses must follow Section 4 of GB 13432-2004. The following labeling information is prohibited:

- Any claims as to alleviation, prevention, or treatment of cure or disease.
- Claims promising longevity, "rejuvenating function," "preventing and curing cancer," "restoring white hair," or their equivalents.
- The use of a drug's name immediately before or after the name of a food or the use of an image and the name of a drug implying functional effects or the treatment of that food. (This does not apply to substances used as both drug and food.)

Label Requirements: Prepackaged Alcoholic Beverages

As in the earlier case, imported prepackaged alcoholic beverages must be labeled in both English and Chinese following the General Standard for the Labeling of Prepackaged Alcoholic Beverages (GB 10344-2005). The General Standard for Beverages (GB 10789-2007) and the General Standard for the Labeling of Prepackaged Foods (GB 7718-2004) are used by the Center of Inspection and Quarantine for the label verification of nonalcoholic beverages.

The following items are an example of the minimum information required. Other information may be required based on the specific product and it is recommended that exporters check with specialist logistic companies or relevant agencies before exporting products to China:

- Wine name and type (e.g., dry write/red, semidry)
- Vintage year
- Grape variety
- Country and wine region
- List of ingredients
- Alcoholic strength
- Name and address of manufacturer and local agent or distributor
- Production date, guidance for storing, and shelf life

- Net weight and volume
- Code of national, enterprise, or industrial standard for the product
- Quality grade
- Production license
- Warning

Label Requirement: Prepackaged Nonalcoholic Beverages

There is no separate standard for labeling for nonalcoholic beverages. The General Standard for Beverages (GB 10789-2007) is used to group beverages but importers can refer to the General Standard for the Labeling of Prepackaged Foods.

Time Frame and Costs

Time Needed for Import Procedures

Costs, like time frames, are never firm and vary according to geographical area. While the cost of an individual license is negligible, the label verification process normally costs around RMB 2,000 in areas like Guangdong and Shanghai but can vary at other ports. Factors such as daily charges for goods housed at Customs, uncertainty over the exact number of goods selected for inspection and sampling, and variable fees for other procedures result in differing costs for each shipment. Import agencies normally charge RMB 2,000 to 3,000 per shipment and about RMB 600 for the design of Chinese labels. The export of health foods, in particular, is expensive. An application for the Imported Health Food Approval Certificate costs RMB 160,000 to 310,000. Agencies will charge around RMB 80,000 to manage the whole process. Although time frames and costs might appear arbitrary at first, they can be reduced by familiarity with the procedures and attention to meeting stated requirements.

Cosmetics

Labels can either be attached to the product or provided in a separate booklet. Labels must contain information on ingredients, amount of each ingredient, and the name and address of the manufacturer and the local distributor.

Electronics

Labels must fulfill the energy label and the restricted use of hazardous substances label requirements.

Chemicals

Imported chemicals and products containing chemicals must be classified, labeled, and packaged according to the globally harmonized system of classification and labeling of chemicals (GHS) as adopted by the United Nations.

Voluntary Labeling

China's voluntary labels are designed to indicate that a product is safe and environmentally friendly. They normally only benefit domestic companies. So far, only large multinational companies have managed to acquire voluntary labels.

Voluntary Labeling

Voluntary labeling schemes are designed to encourage safe, environmentally friendly, and efficient production processes and to foster "green awareness" among Chinese consumers. These labels mainly benefit Chinese companies. Among international companies only large multinationals have so far shown interest in acquiring local voluntary labels. These labels help them in accessing the procurement market for which smaller foreign businesses would rarely qualify. Although confidence is increasing, the market continues to question the authority of Chinese certifications and labels. International system certifications and labels remain the most effective ones globally and in the Chinese market. The main incentive for using voluntary labels when entering the Chinese market is to gain access to the government procurement market.

Incentives for Western businesses are limited but they do exist. The reason they are often limited is that local businesses and consumers have greater confidence in international eco-labels. Furthermore, China-certified labels enjoy little influence among consumers and businesses. If your company can get such a label, it will be a plus but you will gain more advantages if you expend resources in gaining internationally recognized label certifications.

Government Procurement

For Chinese and foreign companies, being on the government procurement list, facilitated by voluntary label and certifications, improves their overall market status in terms of government procurement and, to a certain extent, the appeal of their products to the general consumer.

The Chinese government supports sustainable products by maintaining a green procurement list. In 2019 they spent about RMB 15 billion on listed products, which constitutes only 2 percent of total government procurement. However, where green options were available, more than 60 percent of government-procured products were "green." Only products with government-approved voluntary labels and certifications can be listed. Such companies need to operate at a scale and at competitive levels on which most foreign start-ups and businesses would be unlikely to compete. International companies currently included on government procurement lists are of the scale of HP, Siemens, and DELL.

Tax Concessions

Voluntary labels help Chinese companies earn tax concessions, especially for R&D. For instance, companies active in green sectors, such as researching energy conservation, eco-technology, or even water recycling, are eligible for such concessions. New regulations which are part of the 13th Five-Year Plan have extended these concessions. These new regulations aim to foster indigenous innovation within Chinese domestic companies rather than support Western imports.

Business Management

By improving production and management processes, system certifications help businesses to operate more efficiently and profitably. The label certification process is rather expensive for Chinese companies and requires them to demonstrate their viability. Certification labels are often considered a good measure of the current and future strength of a company. Consumers and business partners are reassured by authoritative eco-labeling.

Consumer Awareness

In industries such as F&B, health, or pharmaceutical products, where food and product safety is a priority, consumers place a higher value on internationally certified products than Chinese ones.

Evolution and Usage of Voluntary Marks and Labeling

The good news is that voluntary certification is still immature in China but interest is quickly increasing.

Labels can be divided into three main categories, based on the duration and cost of the certification process that is required.

- General products
- Food and natural products
- System certifications

General Products

Voluntary product labels which certify green, energy-saving, and water-conservation products are listed next. Food and product safety concerns have propelled a very rapid increase in the number of voluntarily certified products in these categories.

Product Labels

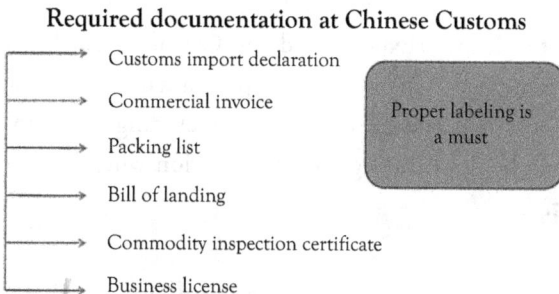

Required documentation at Chinese Customs

Customs import declaration

Commercial invoice

Packing list

Bill of landing

Commodity inspection certificate

Business license

Proper labeling is a must

Common GB standards for labeling of food products:

GB 7718 2011
General Rules for the Labeling of Prepackaged Foods

GB 7718 2004
The General Standard for the Labeling of prepackaged food

GB 13432 2013
General rules for the labeling of prepackaged food for special dietary use

GB 28050-2011
National Food Safety Standards for General Rules for Nutrition Labeling of Prepackaged Food

Common GB standards for labeling of wine and beer:

GB 10344
Labeling guidelines for prepackaged beverage

GB 7718-2011
General Standard for the labeling of prepackaged foods

GB 10344-2005
General Standard for the labeling of prepackaged alcoholic beverages

General national regulations for wine and beverages:

AQSIQ's Order 27 of 2012
Issued for labeling of prepackaged food and wine

AQSIQ's Announcement 59 (2011)
Used for label registration of products that are imported for the first time

AQSIQ's Announcement No. 44 (2006)
Adjustment of Import/Export Food and Cosmetic Label Examination System: Removes separate and preliminary examinations of labels for imported and exported food, including wine. Instead, the approval will be done during CIQ's inspection when the goods arrive at the port.

Natural Products and Food

Interest in certified healthy food products is growing very fast but Chinese consumers' understanding of organic growing practices is still nascent. In Chinese language, the name of the "pollution-free" label sounds more environmentally friendly than the "organic" label, which adds to the confusion. A relatively large number of domestic companies meet the basic requirements or Pollution-free Certification, fewer companies hold Green Food Certification labels, and an even smaller number hold Organic Product labels. If your company sells natural products or food, it is always best to apply for such labels. The most useful label is the Organic Product Certification, as the Pollution-free and Green Food certifications do not indicate sufficient quality to be of benefit to local food importers.

System Certifications

Chinese system certifications are based on the ISO system. Chinese companies have shown strong interest in these international certifications. Only the most likely certified bodies are quoted, as in regional areas CNAS has accredited some smaller agencies. Their labels differ slightly from those shown earlier.

Label Year Established Logo	Standards	Programme description, eligible products, aad website reference
Quality Management System (QMS)	GB/T19001=ISO9001 TL9000 ISO13	For all industries from food through to elctricity, IT, manufacturing, agriculture, energy, transport. Telecommunication industry Medical devices industry Automotive industry Construction industry
Environmental Management System (EMS)	GB/T24001= ISO14001	Minimize how company operations negatively affect the environment. For all industries from food through to electricity, IT, manufacturing, chemical, agriculture
Occupational Health & Safety Management Sysytem (OSHMS)	GB/T28001= OHSAS18001	An all-encompassing system for implementation and improvement of employees' occupational health and safety. For all industries from food through to electricity, IT, manufacture, chemical, agriculture.
Product Conformity & Safety (HACCP)	HACCP	HACCP is a scientific system for ensuring that a product is produced, procesed, manufactured, prepared and consumed safely. Generally for food (including seafood, milk, cream and butter, animal meat) and pharmaceutical companies.

System Certification Cost and Duration

You can expect most system certifications to cost a small-sized enterprise RMB 10,000 to 20,000 and a medium-sized enterprise RMB 30,000 to 40,000. In certain cases, even though a certification is valid for three to five years, annual renewal payments are required. Annual reviews usually cost one-third of the initial total application cost. Preliminary procedures to prepare for voluntary certifications normally take about six months, and it takes one to two months once the formal application has been submitted for the relevant bodies to issue a certificate.

Western businesses familiar with international application and inspection procedures will find that the process in China is in line with international conventions. Procedures vary based on the specific products. The system certification is very similar to that for product label certification. The exact documentation that is required will differ based on the certification. Sellers, importers, and manufacturers are eligible to submit an application.

Additional fees may include:

- Travel and accommodation costs for inspectors
- Cost of every individual label pasted on each product
- Related product examinations
- Extra fees for examination of more complicated company production processes
- Preliminary procedures including hiring a consultancy to help establish a system
- The cost of preliminary/pilot tests

Retail Channels

Promotion Strategies

Women have become a special target group for many retailers, particularly in the first-tier cities, and 35 percent in second-tier cities seek and follow lifestyle information accessed via the Internet. At the same time, traditional media such as television, magazines, newspapers, direct mail, and advertising continue to play an important role in reaching female consumers. For instance, recipes published in local magazines and segments on cooking shows can be instrumental in expanding home-cooking styles. There is also a growing number of gourmet enthusiasts who share information tips and recipes through microblogs. Search engine optimization and online retailing to reach these segments are a potentially fruitful avenue for the promotion of Western products. At the same time, media advertising, especially local TV channels and radio, can be expensive and may not even target the intended audience, but foreign boutique producers and local organic growers with foreign connections have found it rather easy to generate excitement about their products features in the press and other free advertising methods.

Major trade shows, such as FHC and SIAL, provide good opportunities for businesses to test the interest and potential local demand for their products among thousands of visitors to the shows as well as meetings with potential importers and distributors. In this type of shows, most European and American countries organized national pavilions for exporters to display their products.

In addition to marketing and advertising strategies, some major companies and even government organizations have increased awareness of Western food and beverage products through food festivals and sales promotions within shopping malls, supermarkets, or hotels.

As an example, the Agricultural Trade Office (ATO) of the U.S. Consulate General in Shanghai co-organizes annual American food festivals in large cities of China. Promotions are held in five-star hotels to promote U.S. meat products, oysters, snow crabs, potatoes, cheese, raisins, nuts, and other food ingredients. Celebrity chefs are usually present in such events, hosting cooking demos and seminars with local chefs. Italian, Canadian, and British food festivals have also been organized and these events provide great opportunities for countries and companies to showcase their products and services to thousands of increasingly affluent consumers.

Local Partners

When you will start doing business in or with China, you will realize how important it is to have local Chinese partners. A popular way many Western companies use to sell their products in China is through local agents or local distributors. A local agent will be your company's direct representative on the ground and is usually paid a commission and sometimes a basic salary. A local distributor buys your products and then sells them to customers through third parties. For small- and medium-sized companies, using a well-known distributor or agent is one of the easiest ways to sell their products in China mainly because Chinese agents possess the distribution networks, the knowledge, and most importantly the right contacts. They can help overcome cultural and language barriers before promoting and selling your products locally.

In addition, sales and distribution agents can collect market data, help with tracking policy and regulatory updates, and efficiently respond to new developments. However, finding a reliable, dedicated, and professional agent or distributor can be a real challenge. An agent could also be a manufacturer who is in a similar field or an import–export company with well-established connections and an extensive network of suppliers.

Criteria for choosing a good agent or distributor:

- Knowledge of your service/products and its market.
- Previous experience and good references.
- Language skills including English, Mandarin, Cantonese, as well as local dialects.
- Geographical coverage and strong network.
- Staff, support team, subagents.

- Ability to work with incentives (e.g., commission based and subject to customer's payment first).
- Strong work ethic, such as the ability to prepare marketing plans and submit regular reports, translate documents, work with limited marketing budgets, travel, be transparent about any potential conflict of interest, and respect the professional image of the company. For more information on local partners you can refer to my book *Entering the Chinese Market.*

Online Platforms

Selling using online platforms in China is a huge trend which has grown rapidly in the last 10 years. Spurred by the advent of third-party platforms such as Taobao and user-friendly online payment systems such as Alipay, Chinese consumers have become more at ease with e-shopping. As a result, e-commerce has evolved into a readily available distribution channel to access the Chinese market. In fact, distribution through online platforms allows for the promotion of goods to a very vast market, spread across a very large geographic area for a lower cost than physical presence would require. There are four main ways a foreign business can distribute its products online to Chinese consumers:

- Standalone website outside of China
- Standalone website in China
- Third-party platform outside of China
- Third-party platform inside China

Selling online in China will require a well-planned strategy, in terms of website design, SEO, local social media marketing, as well as offline promotional activities to target and engage the right customers.

Franchising

Franchising is another widely used method of distributing services or products. There are at least two levels of people involved in a franchise system: the franchisor, who lends his trademark along with a business system; and the franchisee, who pays an initial fee and a royalty for the right to do business under the franchisor's name. McDonald's and Starbucks are obvious—and very successful—franchising examples in China. When considering franchising, be aware of China's legal framework for commercial franchises. These regulations change often and apply to both domestic and foreign franchisors engaging in commercial franchising in China.

Franchising Requirements

Below you can see a list of the most important requirements for franchise businesses:

- Only companies may engage in franchising as franchisors.
- A franchisor must own a developed business that can provide long-term commitment. as well as technology support, business training, and other services.
- Franchisors must have previous experience in terms of ownership and operation of at least two years before they can establish their own franchise in China.
- In order to act as franchisee, a foreign company must first establish a foreign-invested enterprise in China.

Foreign-Invested Enterprises and Representative Offices

The establishment of a foreign-invested enterprise allows foreign companies more control over the distribution of their product and the management of their corporate image and brand. Depending on the industry and product, the process of setting up a foreign-invested company can be relatively simply or particularly complicated and time-consuming. It is always advisable to first research Chinese regulations in your industry to learn what laws and regulations govern foreign-invested enterprises.

Types of foreign-invested enterprises:

- Wholly foreign-owned enterprise (commonly known as WFOE)
- Equity joint venture (EJV)

- Cooperative joint (CJV)
- Foreign-invested partnership (FIP)
- Representative office (RO)

For more information on these types of foreign-invested enterprises, you may refer to my book *Entering the Chinese Market.*

Wholly Foreign-Owned Enterprises

- The most common form of foreign-invested enterprise in China today.
- An independent limited liability corporation registered with foreign capital under Chinese laws.
- Offers complete control over the business.
- Allows foreign companies to establish an office and own stock without a Chinese partner.
- Establishment process can be cumbersome and time-consuming.
- Appropriate structure for companies whose main China activities are to manufacture and sell products or to provide services such as research and development or business consulting services.

Equity Joint Ventures

- A limited liability corporation established between a Chinese company and a foreign company (or companies).
- The foreign investor must generally hold at least 25 percent of the registered capital.
- Preferred form of foreign-invested enterprise by the Chinese government.
- Jointly held ownership, operations, risks, and rewards.
- Profits are distributed in the form of dividend to the parties based on equity contributions.

Cooperative Joint Ventures

- Established through the partnership between a Chinese business or organization and a foreign enterprise, organization, or individual.
- Can be an incorporated arrangement with a limited liability corporation or a contractual cooperation agreement.
- Ownership of profit and losses is normally not shared based on equity contributions bur rather based on the contractual agreement.
- Provides greater flexibility regarding risk management and profit sharing.

Representative Offices

- Not a legal entity but a liaison office for a foreign company in China
- Not allowed to engage in any profit-making activities on behalf of their foreign headquarters
- Not a viable choice for product distribution in China

Operational Challenges

Working With Chinese Partners

One very common cause of business failure in China is when partnerships have gone sour. Recognizing cultural differences and spending time to understand how your Chinese partner operates are paramount. New entrants to the Chinese market often become frustrated because they perceive that their Chinese partners are neither forthcoming nor frank. They also find that agreements considered as binding by the Western partner are way more flexible or negotiable from the perspective of the Chinese side.

Informal social occasions and formal business meetings are a great opportunity to build trust, receive professional advice, and secure business deals. Ensuring that a representative of your company is present at all transactions helps reduce misunderstandings.

What an Import Contract Should Include

Once you have selected a local partner who will support your goods or services in China, it is necessary to negotiate an import contract. While the content of the contract will depend on the goods to be exported, it is essential to have a binding contract in place whenever exporting goods to China. An importer does not necessarily need to be a buyer. A sales and purchase contract is the most basic and most common form of an import contract. If you are looking to export your products to Chinese importers, you will need to negotiate and agree upon such a contract. A foreign company that carefully negotiates a sales and purchase contract along with dispute resolution mechanisms will greatly reduce the risks of exporting to China.

Fundamentals of a sales and purchase contract

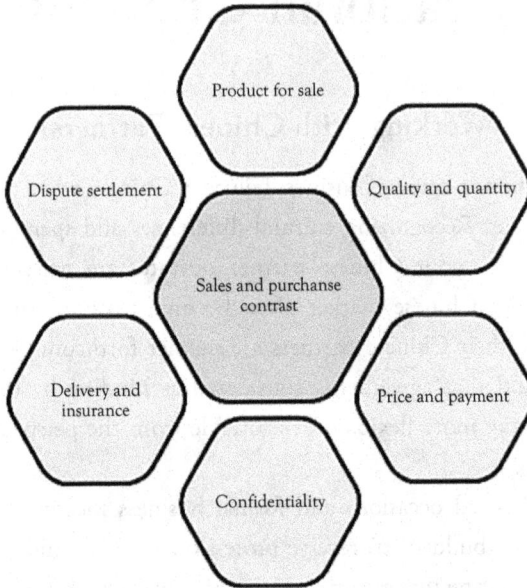

Product for sale

Dispute settlement

Quality and quantity

Sales and purchanse contrast

Delivery and insurance

Price and payment

Confidentiality

Major Components of a Sales and Purchase Contract

Selection of legal jurisdiction. According to the Chinese contract law, when a foreign party enters into a sales and purchase contract with a Chinese party, they can decide whether the contract will be governed by Chinese or foreign law. Although Western companies will usually prefer the laws of their home country, the Chinese party is reluctant to agree.

Clear definition of seller and buyer. Clearly define which parties are bound by the contract.

Contract product. Offer a detailed description of the product or service, so there is no confusion.

Quantity. The quantity as well as the unit used for the measurement of the goods should be specified.

Quality enforcement. A large number of disputes in such contracts arise as a result of product quality issues. To handle these issues, a well-developed and agreed-upon system for product inspection needs to be put into place. Regarding product inspections, the standards and specifications of the products should be included in the sales and purchase contract. Quality maintenance systems usually include the following:

- A sample of the product to be inspected along with the contract
- Preshipment of the product for inspection
- Inspection by the Chinese importer at the port
- Inspection at the final destination by the Chinese importer
- In case of dispute, a final binding inspection by a neutral third party designated by both parties in advance

Price and payment method. The price of the goods must be agreed in advance as well as whether the Chinese party will make the payment in RMB, U.S. dollars, euros, or another currency. It is important to take into account the appreciation trend of the RMB against the U.S. dollar or the Euro when calculating payments. A payment process and timeline must also be included in the contract. Additionally, it is wise to include a list of who will be responsible for what costs associated with the transfer of goods (port charges, import–export fees, tariffs, storage, etc.).

Here it is important to discuss about letters of credit as a payment method. A letter of credit is a written promise to pay and is issued by the Chinese buyer's bank to the Western exporter. The letter guarantees that as long as the Western exporter provides their goods to the Chinese buyer as agreed upon, they will be paid. Even in case the Chinese buyer ultimately fails to pay the Western exporter, their bank will still pay the full amount. Letters of credit are commonly used in large international transactions to reduce the risk of the seller.

Confidentiality. If you are exporting products containing intellectual property, such as trademarks or copyrights, you should include a confidentiality clause in the sales and purchase contract as a way to protect your IP rights. In any case, registration of all IP rights is highly recommended.

Delivery. You will need to provide a specific delivery schedule and decide whether partial shipments will be allowed.

Time of effectiveness. Clearly indicate when the contract will become effective as well as when it will be terminated.

Insurance. It is important to indicate who will be responsible for the insurance of the goods during transport to China, as well as it is important to indicate who will be responsible for after shipping and delivery.

Liability for breach of contract. A clear liability clause should be included for the breach of contract and indicate what actions will be taken if the contract is breached and how the parties will reach a dispute settlement.

Dispute settlement. In case a dispute arises, there are normally two ways to solve it: arbitration or litigation. Under China's Arbitration Law, the parties in conflict must agree on the method to solve a dispute, either litigation or arbitration. They cannot choose both.

If no agreement is made on arbitration, litigation will automatically be resorted to.

Litigation

Litigation is normally expensive and lengthy. A lawsuit involving an international sale and purchase can take more than a year to resolve. Trade secrets or IP may be leaked due to the public nature of some law suits. According to Chinese law, litigation brought against a Chinese legal entity usually has to be resolved where the defendant is registered.

Arbitration

Arbitration is the most common dispute resolution mechanism for sales and purchase contracts in China. It can take place in a third country that is neither China nor your home country. The contract parties are free to select the arbitration institution. To ensure neutrality it is possible to choose an international arbitral body. A simpler procedure will lead to a faster decision.

Foreign Exchange Controls and Limitations

Foreign exchange is the selling and buying of currencies. It is inherent in international transactions. In all import contracts that you will sign, it is important to specify what currency you would like to receive your payments in. Western companies would normally prefer to receive the payment in their local currency for services and products sold in China. Chinese importers will prefer however to pay in RMB. Be aware that foreign exchange risk enters into question every time there is conversion from one currency into another. You can either try to develop a strategy to manage foreign exchange risk based on your company's needs or ask the buyer to complete all transactions in the currency of your home country.

It is very likely that most of the time your Chinese partners will be reluctant to pay for transactions in your home currency, simply because the process for acquiring foreign exchange is especially cumbersome and restrictive in mainland China. As regulated by the State Administration of Foreign Exchange (SAFE), foreign exchange can only be purchased from a few banks only for certain amounts. Because there is a big number of regulations on the use and holding on foreign currencies, it is best to do some research based on your company's activities and your home currency.

Final Thoughts

Below, I have included several points in the form of a SWOT analysis to help you determine the strengths, weaknesses, opportunities, and threats that you may face. The following questions may be helpful in determining what strategy to employ, what potential opportunities exist, and what are the risks linked to them.

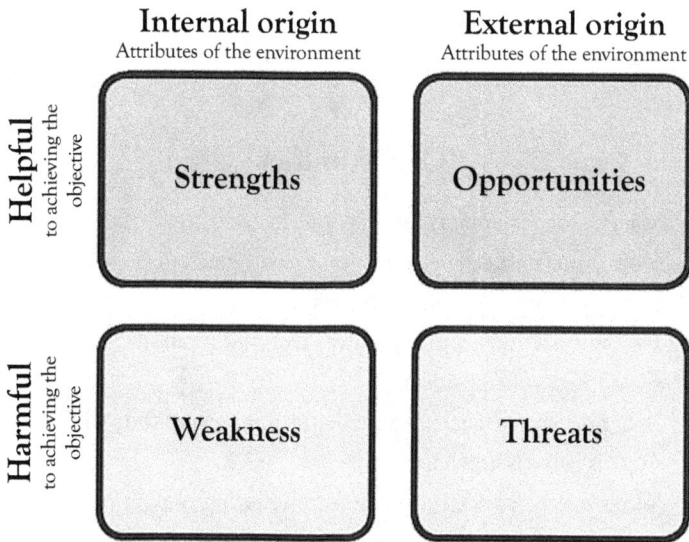

	Internal origin Attributes of the environment	**External origin** Attributes of the environment
Helpful to achieving the objective	**Strengths**	**Opportunities**
Harmful to achieving the objective	**Weakness**	**Threats**

Before entering the Chinese market it is recommended to develop a comprehensive strategy that addresses these essential points:

- What you stand to gain by entering the Chinese market?
- What China stands to gain through your entry?
- What risks are you likely to face?
- How to handle potential risks?

Strengths and Weaknesses

- What is the current level of your product's brand recognition in your home market?
- How capable is your company of adapting its structure and/or practices to fit the China business environment?
- Are your current employees able to manage a transition into China?
- What is your current competitive advantage (in terms of quality, cost, customer service, and so on.)?
- Does your current customer base have a presence in China? If so, can these relationships be leveraged to help in gaining traction?
- What other strengths and weaknesses exist in your organization that need to be addressed while developing a China entry strategy?

Opportunities

- What level of demand for your products currently exists in China?
- Does your market offering coincide with current political agendas, either in China or your home market?
- Do you see any potential for technological improvements to strengthen your position?
- What does your current target consumer group look like? In what ways is it likely to change?
- What is your prime motivation for entering the China market?

Threats

- How will fluctuations in the local and global economy affect your market position in China?
- Do you have a strategy to protect your IP rights (trademarks, patents, copyrights, or trade secrets)?
- Do you have a strategy to manage foreign exchange risk?
- What challenges have your competitors faced and how have they dealt with them?

- What assumptions are you making regarding your motivations for entering the Chinese market? How can you confirm or disprove them?
- Additional issues to consider when entering the Chinese market.

Branding in the Chinese Market

For most Western companies intent on launching in China, one of the main entry barriers is low brand recognition in the local market. A food and beverage or high-tech brand may well be widely known in Europe but it is crucial for the business to position itself suitably within the local market. In order to become a more recognizable brand, many Western companies completely redesigned their corporate identity to fit local tastes. For instance, the Spanish San Gines logo was modified with the addition of a chef and a translation of the brand name in Chinese. This was done to ensure that the brand could be read, pronounced, and, most importantly, remembered by Chinese consumers. Be aware that Chinese costumers place a strong emphasis on branding. They tend to prefer well-established brands which they have heard of. Therefore, building a strong brand is crucial for newcomers in China.

Social Media and Digital Marketing in China

Digital marketing in China is growing at an incredible speed as a way of building brand value through China's social media platforms. Chinese traditional media landscape is fragmented, meaning that traditional advertisements only reach a region or city. However, the good news is that China's social networking scene covers the whole of China. Western social media such as Facebook, Twitter, and YouTube are blocked in China but there are many local equivalents such as Weibo (similar to Twitter), RenRen (similar to Facebook), WeChat (a cross between Facebook and an instant messaging service), and Youku (similar to You-Tube), which are widely used in China, through both the Internet and mobile devices.

Chinese social media are used by most Chinese consumers, thus enabling Western businesses to implement marketing campaigns based on the use of local microblogs. Very often social media-influencing leaders are engaged by companies to post positive comments and reviews on their behalf. A positive word of mouth recommendation spread through these social media can make or break the launch of a new product or service. If these tools are utilized effectively, they can be a low-cost alternative to traditional brand enhancement and advertising.

If you wish to know more about selling and advertising in the Chinese online market, you may refer to my book *Entering the Chinese e-Merging Market* by Business Expert Press.

China offers plenty of opportunities for Western businesses. Before you go any further, make sure you follow these basic steps:

RESEARCH is paramount before entering any new market, but China's distance from Europe and the United States, its complexity, and size make it a unique challenge. Just imagine a country as large and diverse as Europe and Russia are combined and you begin to get the picture. The opportunities are too promising to ignore, while the risk of a failed market entry can be especially high. At the same time, quality market research for China is something that the average business—or even the average market research company—cannot do. Many companies do less advance research than they would when launching their products into their home markets, and are therefore doomed to fail. Don't be one of them! Make sure you hire specialist help whenever needed and explore all options available to your particular business and industry segment. Independent guidance, and focused research, is what you need to make the right decisions for your business.

REGISTRATION of your intellectual property rights in China should be done as early as possible. China has a "first-come first-served" system, so if someone else registers your trademark before you do, they have the legal right to them. So, it's crucial to get help from a China IP law specialist.

Now it might be the right time to ask whether your current names and logos are suitable for China or not. What should they be? Some English words and names are hard to write and even pronounce in Chinese, or they may carry an unintended meaning because of their sound. Local branding specialists can help you with this sort of issues and assist you with name choices and logo designs.

RETHINK both your product/service and marketing strategy in the light of your market research. No matter how your product is viewed by customers elsewhere in the world, do not assume that it will get the same reception in China.

RESILIENCE will be needed if you are to tackle China properly. Building business and partner relations there takes time, and drawbacks are definitely to be expected. Despite China having a strong infrastructure and a relatively stable political system, the country has been rated "high" for legal and regulatory risk and "high" for labor market risk. Both of these can hurt pretty hard, especially in the first couple of years of your market entry, as you will most likely have to deal with import licenses, unfamiliar tax systems, business registration procedures, and remote employees. You must prepare for these by getting good professional advice upfront, which will help you set expectations—and budgets—wisely.

RELATIONSHIPS—the famous "guanxi"—are crucial when doing business in and with China. Take note of this! Chinese prefer to do business with trusted friends and this very fact has many implications for business strategy. As an example, you should budget for senior managers to visit potential partners or clients in China more than once before any significant sales are expected to be made. And that's just scratching the surface! You must also be ready for events such as business trips and hosting delegations.

You may need to find an agent or distributor, and getting the right one for your specific target market and product could be the difference between sales generation and sales frustration. Once again there are many options available. Make sure the agent is capable of building the right connections and that they set up quality distributor arrangements.

Finally, *be READY!* It may well be that China comes looking for you before you are even prepared.

China's world trade in numbers

China's Worldwide Reach
The Western Hemisphere has become the focus of attention for Chinese companies.

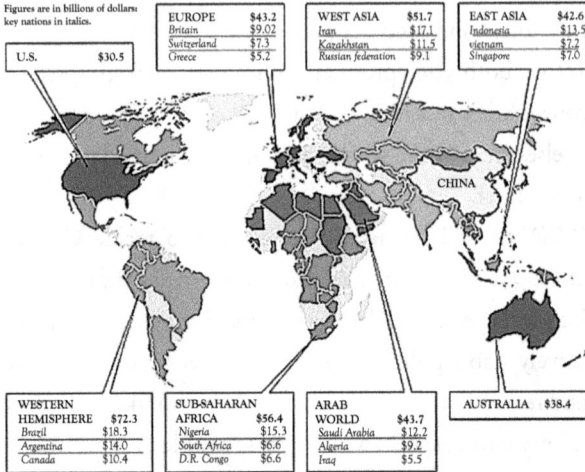

Figures are in billions of dollars; key nations in italics.

EUROPE	$43.2
Britain	$9.02
Switzerland	$7.3
Greece	$5.2

WEST ASIA	$51.7
Iran	$17.1
Kazakhstan	$11.5
Russian federation	$9.1

EAST ASIA	$42.6
Indonesia	$13.5
vietnam	$7.2
Singapore	$7.0

U.S. $30.5

CHINA

WESTERN HEMISPHERE	$72.3
Brazil	$18.3
Argentina	$14.0
Canada	$10.4

SUB-SAHARAN AFRICA	$56.4
Nigeria	$15.3
South Africa	$6.6
D.R. Congo	$6.6

ARAB WORLD	$43.7
Saudi Arabia	$12.2
Algeria	$9.2
Iraq	$5.5

AUSTRALIA	$38.4

Cumulative value of Chinese FDI transactions in the EU by country, 2000-2019
EUR billion

- 0–5
- 5–10
- 10–20
- 20–40
- >40

Sweden 7.3
Finland 12.0
Estonia 0.1
Latvia 0.1
Lithuania 0.1
Ireland 3.1
Denmark 1.2
UK 50.3
Netherlands 10.2
Poland 1.4
Belgium 2.3
Germany 22.7
Luxembourg 2.4
Czech Republic 1.0
Slovakia 0.1
France 14.4
Austria 1.1
Hungary 2.4
Slovenia 0.3
Romania 1.2
Croatia 0.4
Portugal 6.0
Spain 4.6
Italy 15.9
Bulgaria 0.4
Greece 1.9
Malta 0.8
Cyprus 0.2

Source: Rhodium Group.

Source: Rhodium Group

China's Biggest Exports
Total Value of China's Exports by Country

Netherlands
$73B

United
Kingdom
$57B

Ireland
$4B

Norway Sweden Finland
$3B $8B $3B

Estonia $1B
Latvia $1B
Lithuania $2B

Denmark
$7B

Poland
$21B

Belarus $1B

Slovakia
$3B

Hungary Ukraine
$8B $7B

Russia
$48B

Kazakhstan
$11B

Kyrgys Rep.
$6B

Czech Rep. $7B

Austria $12B

Romania $4B
Slovenia $4B
Bulgaria $5B

Uzbekistan
$3B

Tajikistan
$1B

Mongolia
$2B

DPR Korea
$2B

South
Korea
$110B

Japan
$148B

Germany
$78B

France
$17B

Belgium
$18B

Switzerland
$4B

Italy
$33B

Croatia $1B

Greece
$7B

Georgia
$1B

Turkey
$18B

Iran
$14B

Pakistan
$17B

Nepal $1B

India
$77B

Hong
Kong
$304B

Taiwan
$49B

Spain
$25B

Malta
$1B

Lebanon
$2B

Syria
$1B

Jordan
$2B

Israel
$3B

Iraq
$8B

Kuwait
$1B

Bahrain
$1B Qatar
$1B UAE
$30B

Oman
$3B

Myanmar
$11B

Vietnam
$84B

Laos
$1B

Macao
$3B

Portugal
$4B

Morocco
$4B

Tunisia
$1B

Libya $1B

Egypt
$12B

Mauritania $1B

Algeria
$8B

Sudan
$2B

Saudi
Arabia
$9B

Djibouti Yemen
$2B $2B

Cambodia
$6B

Bangladesh
$18B

Sri
Lanka
$4B

Thailand
$43B

Singapore
$50B

Senegal
$2B

Guinea
$1B

Liberia
$2B

Cote
d'Ivoire $2B

Togo $2B

Nigeria
$2B

Benin
$2B

Cameroon
$3B

Ethiopia
$3B

DR Congo
$2B

Kenya
$5B

Tanzania
$4B

Oman
$3B

Philippines
$35B

Marshall Is.
$2B

Brunei
Darussalam
$2B

Indonesia
$43B

Malaysia
$46B

Australia
$48B

New Zealand
$6B

Angola
$2B

Mozambique
$2B

Madagascar
$1B

South Africa
$16B

U.S.
$481B

Canada
$36B

Mexico
$44B

Guatemala
$2B

Costa Rica
$2B

Panama
$7B

Dominican
Rep.

Cuba
$1B

Colombia
$9B

Ecuador
$4B

Peru
$9B

Venezuela
$5B

Brazil
$34B

Paraguay
$2B

Uruguay
$2B

Chile
$16B

Argentina
$8B

China's Exports 2018 ($)

$100B and More

$50B - $99.9B

$10B - $49.9B

$1B - $9.9B

Note: This visualization
shows countries where
China has $1 billion or
more in exports.

How to read this map: Size and color of the countries correspond to the value of China's exports to those countries.
Countries appear bigger and darker as the value of China's exports to those countries is higher. E.g. United States.

China's Biggest Imports
Total Value of China's Imports by Country

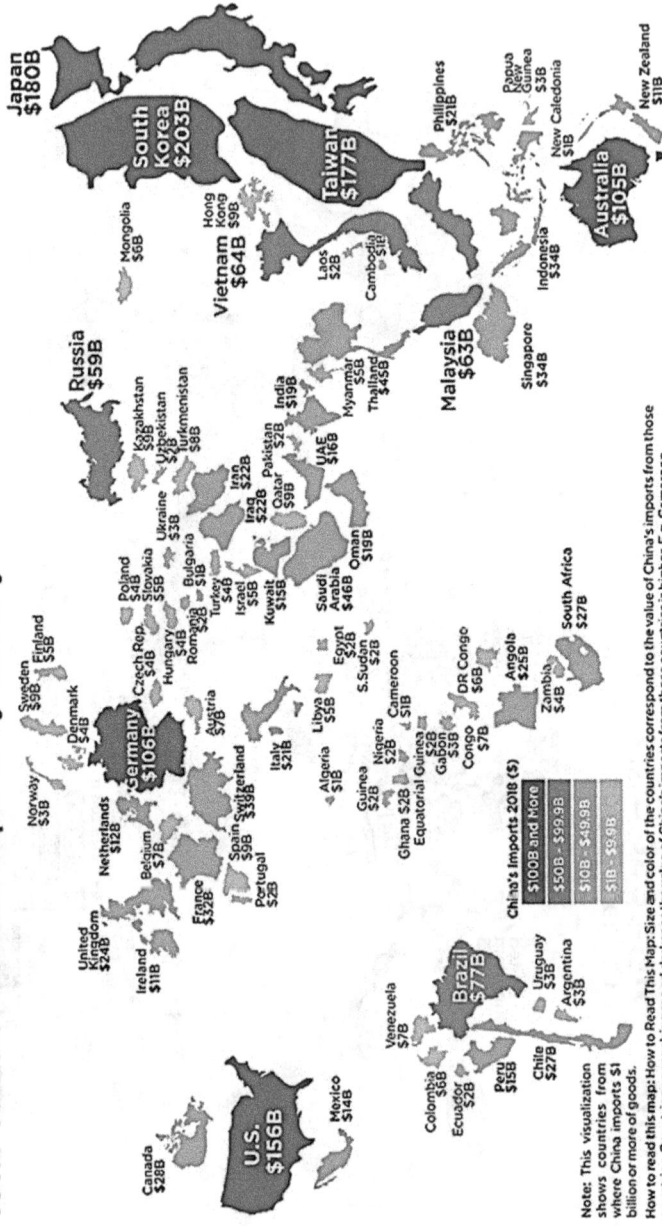

Japan $180B

South Korea $203B

Taiwan $177B

Vietnam $64B

Hong Kong $9B

Mongolia $6B

Philippines $21B

Papua New Guinea $3B

New Caledonia $1B

New Zealand $11B

Australia $105B

Indonesia $34B

Laos $2B

Cambodia $1B

Russia $59B

Kazakhstan $9B

Uzbekistan $7B

Turkmenistan $8B

India $19B

Pakistan $2B

Myanmar $5B

Thailand $45B

Singapore $34B

Malaysia $63B

Iran $12B

Iraq $22B

Qatar $9B

UAE $16B

Saudi Arabia $46B

Oman $19B

Kuwait $15B

Poland $4B

Slovakia $5B

Czech Rep. $4B

Ukraine $3B

Hungary $4B

Bulgaria $1B

Romania $2B

Turkey $4B

Israel $5B

Sweden $9B

Finland $5B

Denmark $4B

Germany $106B

Austria $4B

Switzerland $39B

Norway $3B

Netherlands $12B

Belgium $7B

France $32B

Spain $9B

Italy $21B

Portugal $2B

United Kingdom $24B

Ireland $11B

Algeria $5B

Libya $5B

Egypt $2B

S. Sudan $2B

Cameroon $1B

Nigeria $2B

Ghana $2B

Guinea $2B

Equatorial Guinea $1B

Gabon $3B

Congo $7B

DR Congo $6B

Zambia $4B

Angola $25B

South Africa $27B

Venezuela $7B

Colombia $6B

Ecuador $2B

Peru $15B

Chile $27B

Brazil $77B

Uruguay $3B

Argentina $3B

Canada $28B

U.S. $156B

Mexico $14B

China's Imports 2018 ($)
$100B and More
$50B - $99.9B
$10B - $49.9B
$1B - $9.9B

Note: This visualization shows countries from where China imports $1 billion or more of goods.

How to read this map: How to Read This Map: Size and color of the countries correspond to the value of China's imports from those countries. Countries appear bigger and darker as the value of China's imports from those countries is higher. E.g. Cameroon.

China's Trade Balance
China's Biggest Trade Deficits/Surpluses by Country

China's Trade Deficit ($)   China's Trade Surplus ($)

| $100B and More | $50B – $99.9B | $10B – $49.9B | $1B – $9.9B | $1B – $9.9B | $10B – $49.9B | $50B – $99.9B | $100B and More |

Netherlands $61B

United Kingdom $33B
Ireland $7B

Canada $7B

U.S. $324B
Mexico $10B
Dominican Rep. $2B
Guatemala $2B
Panama $7B
Colombia $3B
Ecuador $2B
Peru $7B
Venezuela $6B
Brazil $44B
Paraguay $2B
Chile $11B Argentina $5B

Denmark $2B Finland $2B Lithuania $1B
Germany $28B Czech Rep. $6B **Poland $17B**
France $1B Austria $1B Slovakia $3B
Belgium $10B Slovenia $1B Hungary $3B Ukraine $4B
Switzerland $35B Croatia $1B Romania $2B
Spain $16B Greece $6B Bosnia $2B Georgia $1B
Portugal $2B Italy $12B **Turkey $4B** Jordan $1B
Malta $1B Lebanon $2B Israel $2B Syria $3B Kuwait $12B
Morocco $3B Tunisia $1B Yemen $5B Qatar $7B
Senegal $2B Algeria $1B Libya $3B **Egypt $10B** Sudan $1B Djibouti $2B Oman $16B
Liberia $2B Togo $2B Benin $2B S. Sudan $1B Ethiopia $2B
Côte d'Ivoire $2B Ghana $2B **Nigeria $12B** DR Congo $4B Kenya $6B
Equatorial Guinea $2B Gabon $3B Congo $6B Tanzania $1B
Angola $23B Zambia $3B Mozambique $1B
South Africa $11B

Kazakhstan $3B
Uzbekistan $1B Kyrgyz Rep.
Turkmenistan $8B Tajikistan $1B
Pakistan $15B
Iraq $14B Iran $8B
UAE $14B
Saudi Arabia $28B
India $58B
Nepal $1B Sri Lanka $4B

Russia $11B
Mongolia $5B
Hong Kong $295B
DPR Korea $2B
South Korea $93B
Japan $3B
Macao $3B
Bangladesh $17B Myanmar $6B
Cambodia $6B
Thailand $2B
Vietnam $20B
Taiwan $128B
Philippines $15B
Brunei Darussalam $1B
Malaysia $17B
Singapore $16B
Indonesia $9B
Marshall Is. $2B
Papua New Guinea $5B
Australia $57B
New Zealand $5B

Note: This visualization shows countries with a trade balance with China higher than $1B.

How to read this map: Size and color of the countries correspond to the value of trade balance with China. Countries appear in pink color if China imports more from these countries than it exports to the same. Countries appear bigger and darker pink as the value of China's imports from those countries is higher. E.g. Taiwan. Countries appear in turquoise color if China exports more to those countries than it imports from the same. Countries appear bigger and darker turquoise as the value of China's exports to those countries is higher. E.g. United States.

China Free Trade Zone

● 2013   ● 2015   ● 2016   ● 2018   ● 2019

Liaoning

Shaanxi
Henan
Hubei
Chongqing
Sichuan
Zhejiang

Yunnan

Guangxi

Heilongjiang

Hebei
Tianjin
Shandong
Jiangsu
Shanghai

Fujian
Guangdong

Hainan

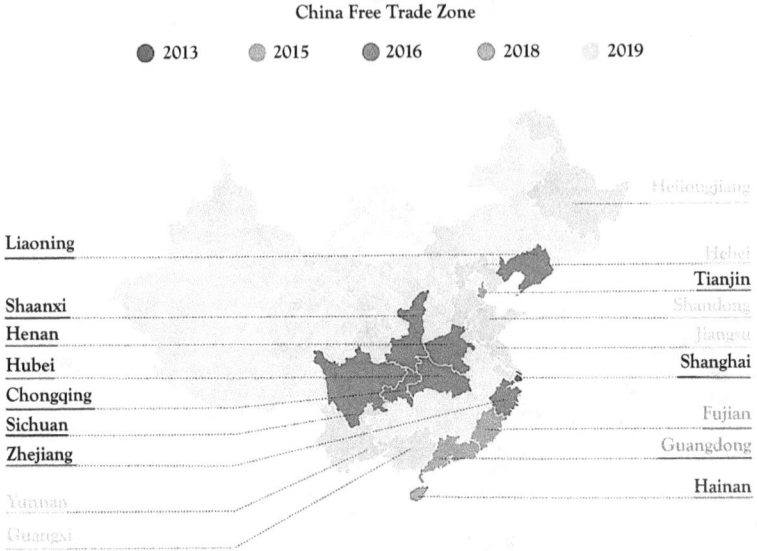

World: Export dependence on China

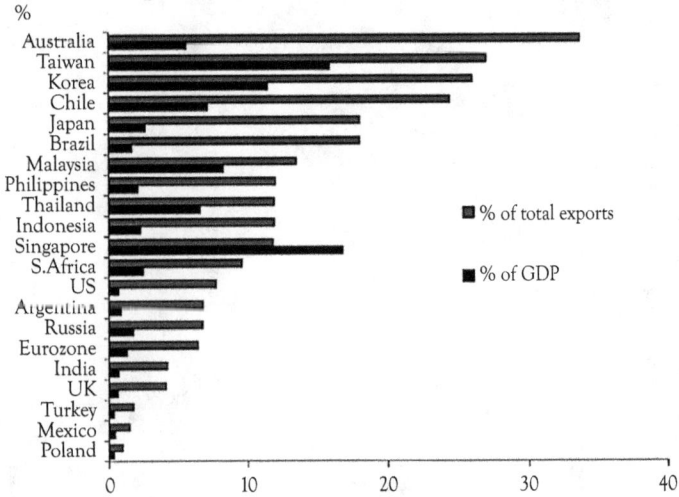

%

Australia
Taiwan
Korea
Chile
Japan
Brazil
Malaysia
Philippines
Thailand
Indonesia
Singapore
S.Africa
US
Argentina
Russia
Eurozone
India
UK
Turkey
Mexico
Poland

■ % of total exports

■ % of GDP

0   10   20   30   40

Source: Oxford Economics/Haver Analytics

Useful Links and References

Useful Websites
Administration of Quality Supervision, Inspection and Quarantine (AQSIQ) www.aqsiq.net/
Chinese Academy of Inspection and Quarantine www.caiq.org.cn/eng/
China Food and Drug Administration www.sfdachina.com/
Certification and Accreditation Administration of the People's Republic of China (CNCA) www.cnca.gov.cn
PRC—General Administration of Customs http://english.customs.gov.cn/
U.S.–China Business Council www.uschina.org/
China–Britain Business Council http://cbbc.org/
EU Commission: DG Trade http://trade.ec.europa.eu/doclib
United Kingdom–Department for International Trade–China www.great.gov.uk/markets/china/
Chinese Ministry of Information and Industry (MIIT) The latest statistics on China's ICT and telecommunications industries www.miit.gov.cn
China Internet Network Information Centre The latest statistics on Internet usage in China http://cnnic.net.cn/en/index/

Amcham/American Chamber of Commerce in China **www.amchamchina.org**
European Union Chamber of Commerce in China **www.eusmecenter.org**
McKinsey Global Institute Analysis **www.mckinsey.com**
IResearch China **www.iresearchchina.com**
China Internet Watch **www.chinainternetwatch.com**
Global Sources **www.globalsources.com**
Hannover Research **www.hanoverresearch.com**

Key Industry Exhibitions and Promotional Events

International Technology Fair—Shanghai World Expo

The International Technology Fair covers innovation-driven development, intellectual property protection, and trade technology. It aims to actively build an authoritative display, exchange, and service platform that promotes the development of trade technology and the execution of an innovation strategy by integrating scientific and technological innovation achievements in China and abroad.

China Robot Show—Beijing International Exhibition Center

The China Robot Show is China's only national, international, and professional robotic intelligence exhibition. It is the largest and most authoritative robot event in the Asia-Pacific region. The exhibition brings together all kinds of industrial robots, service robots, smart cars, VR technology, and comprehensive robotic intelligence industry exhibition and provides a strong platform for brand promotion and channel expansion. A major event for the new robotic intelligence market worldwide.

Shanghai International Clean Technology and Equipment Exhibition

The Beijing International Smart City Expo is the most influential professional exhibition in the smart city industry in China and Asia. The exhibition is cosponsored by the Ministry of Commerce of the People's Republic of China, the Ministry of Science and Technology, the State Intellectual Property Office, and the Shanghai Municipal People's Government.

Beijing International Aerospace Technology and Equipment Exhibition

The International Aerospace Technology and Equipment Exhibition is one of the theme exhibition areas of China National Defense Information Technology Equipment and Technology Expo. The total area of this exhibition exceeds 20,000 square meters with 600 standard booths, creating the world's most professional aerospace industry event.

Beijing International Smart City Expo

The Beijing International Smart City Expo is the most influential professional exhibition in the smart city industry in China and Asia. The exhibition is cosponsored by the Ministry of Commerce of the People's Republic of China, the Ministry of Science and Technology, the State Intellectual Property Office, and the Shanghai Municipal People's Government. The exhibition showcases new smart city construction techniques and solutions. New technologies, new products, and the latest solutions in the field of smart city construction with demonstration and applications, including smart industries and future technologies, future life, and interactive experiences.

China Yiwu International Exhibition for Digital Printing Technology & Application

The China Yiwu International Exhibition for Digital Printing Technology & Application offers the attendees the opportunity to explore the exhibits of digital printing machine, thermal/cold transfer printing machine, flat/rotary screen printing machine, automatic platform printing machine, ink and materials, and related printing software, design, and products.

China International Internet of Things Exhibition—Shenzhen

The China International Internet of Things Exhibition is the largest and most comprehensive IoT expo in Asia. It exhibits the technologies of RFID, sensor network, short-range communication, financial payment, middle-ware, big data processing, Cloud, real-time localization, and so on. It also shows the IoT solutions and applications in various industries, such as transportation, manufacturing, smart grid, smart home, logistics, anti-counterfeiting, attendance, military, asset management, apparel, library, smart city, environment monitoring, IoT perceptual layer (RFID, barcode, smart card, smart sensor), transport network layer (NB-IoT, LoRa, 2G/3G/4G/5G, eSIM, Bluetooth, WIFI, GPS, UWB), and intelligent applications layer (Cloud, RTLS, New Retail, Industry 4.0, Smart logistics, Smart City, Smart Home).

AT & IT—Pharma Automation & Informatization

AT & IT—Pharma Automation & Informatization offers a smart space for bringing together popular products in the field of medical automation and informationization and organizes a three-day medical automation and informationization theme forum with professional associations and alliances to meet the current pharmaceutical production capacity upgrade needs.

Shanghai International Import and Export Food & Beverage Exhibition (FBIE)

The Shanghai International Import and Export Food & Beverage Exhibition (FBIE) is an international platform for food and beverage brands. The FBIE is a grand purchasing meeting for domestic and overseas F&B enterprises and provides a green channel and a strong platform for overseas F&B enterprises to enter the Chinese market. At the same time, the exhibition helps Chinese suppliers and producers to expand to international markets.

FHC China 2020, Shanghai New International Centre (SNIEC)

This is one of China's most important business events for the global food and hospitality sector. Companies from the hospitality, food, drink, foodservice, bakery, and retail industries from many Asian and Western countries participate in this event. FHC China is the leading comprehensive exhibition platform in China. Its main exhibits include seafood, high-end dairy products and oils, tea and coffee, bakery and gelato, snacks, confectionary and chocolate, high-end food supply chain, catering design and decoration, and so on.

SIAL China 2020 , Shanghai New International Centre (SNIEC)

SIAL is one of Asia's leading professional food and beverage exhibition held in Shanghai. SIAL China is an integral part of the SIAL Network, the world's largest network of food and drink fairs. In 2020, SIAL China celebrated its 20th anniversary. The show sets the benchmark for overseas companies stepping into Asia and China and offers valuable market insights, trends, and innovations of the regional food industry. It has become Asia's largest F&B innovation exhibition.

Food and Beverage Online

www.21food.com/

This is a global food e-marketplace/platform for buyers and suppliers to find partners or products to do business with online.

Beijing International Smart Agriculture Equipment and Technology Expo

The Beijing International Smart Agriculture Equipment and Technology Expo focuses on Silk Road Cooperation and Win-Win-Closed Matchmaking Meeting in the Reclamation Area. This exhibition gathers authoritative experts from the Chinese Academy of Engineering, Chinese Academy of Agricultural Sciences, and National Agricultural Technology Extension Service Center and other industry experts coming to discuss the key trends and future of the industry.

Beijing International Wisdom Agricultural Equipment and Technology Exhibition

Exhibition size: 33 countries and regions, 800 standard booths, 25,000 m² of exhibition area, and 35,000 professional visitors. The exhibition is held together with the "China Intelligent Agriculture Innovation and Development Summit Forum" and "China Water Saving Irrigation Industry Summit Forum" and is combined with other on-site activities. The exhibition invites well-known experts from the industry to gather and engage in creative discussions around the topic of intelligent agriculture. The organizing committee arranges visits and exchanges between international professional buyers while also organizing domestic provincial agricultural demonstration parks and high-tech agricultural industrial parks.

IT & CM China

IT & CM China brings together Chinese and International MICE exhibitors and buyers in one dynamic marketplace. IT & CM China is the platform for international and leading Chinese players in the MICE industry to explore business opportunities on all fronts: inbound, outbound, and domestic.

Shanghai International Wheel Exhibition

The Shanghai International Wheel Exhibition is a professional wheel industry trade show. Leading industry enterprises display the latest achievements in the field of wheel processing, such as wheel materials and equipment. A wide range of activities also take place during the fair to provide participants with a professional, authoritative, international exchange platform to discuss new products, new materials, new equipment, new technologies, new concepts, and future development trends of the automotive wheel industry.

China International Vehicle Lighting Technology Exhibition

The exhibition focuses on the latest technology applications in the industry, comprehensively covering the entire industrial chain of the automotive lamp and vehicle lighting industry and meeting the procurement needs of professional buyers to the greatest extent. It sets up a convenient communication arena for OEMs, modification shops, and manufacturers. The latest products and technologies, including vehicle lighting systems, lights, light sources, equipment, materials, testing agencies, development tools, and molds, are exhibited. Brands, products, technologies, and concepts from the United States, Germany, Japan, South Korea, and other countries are invited to promote their products and share their success stories and experience of international product management.

International Photovoltaic Power Generation and Smart Energy Conference & Exhibition

The International Photovoltaic Power Generation and Smart Energy Conference & Exhibition (SNEC PV POWER EXPO) provides the attendees with the opportunity to explore the exhibit of PV manufacturing facilities, materials, PV cells, PV application products and modules, and PV project and system, covering every section of the whole PV industry chain.

China International Medical Equipment Fair

The China International Medical Equipment Fair displays products such as medical imaging, IVD equipment, medical electronics, medical optics, first aid, rehabilitation devices, nursing, telemedicine, wearable devices, and outsourcing services, and it serves the entire value chain of medical devices.

China International Exhibition of Senior Care, Rehabilitation Medicine & Healthcare

CHINA AID is the leading exhibition for the fast developing senior care market in China. It enjoys a firmly established reputation as the most authoritative industry trade show in the country. Taking place annually in Shanghai, the show offers an unparalleled opportunity to meet with prospective clients and customers, partners and distributors, buyers and decision makers from across China. Boasting more than 330 participating exhibitors, a floor space exceeding 25,000 m² and an attendance of over 43,000 visitors, CHINA AID is focused on six category areas, showcasing the latest service, product, and technology offerings in rehabilitation, senior care, nursing care, assertive devices, and age-friendly housing and health care management.

China (Shanghai) International Medical Devices Exhibition

The C-Medical Fair covers comprehensive products, including medical electronic products, medical imaging equipment, ward nursing and auxiliary equipment, medical supplies and hygienic materials, testing equipment and diagnostic reagents, optical products, first-aid products, rehabilitation nursing products, as well as health information technology, providing direct and comprehensive service to the medical devices industry, from the source to the terminal, covering the entire medical industrial chain.

China International Dental Exhibition & Scientific Conference

The China International Dental Exhibition & Scientific Conference (Sino-Dental) aims to provide a platform for national and international dental companies to showcase their products and services. It provides opportunities for the exhibitors and professionals to communicate and exchange their industry experience. It has played an active role in promoting dental technology progress and enjoys a high reputation both in China and around the Asia-Pacific region.

Medical Beauty and Plastic Surgery Equipment Exhibition

The Medical Beauty and Plastic Surgery Equipment Exhibition event showcases products such as medical plastic surgery appliances and equipment, slimming equipment, treadmills, fitness massage, fitness massage belt, ultrasound liposuction instruments, and many more related products and services.

China International Medical Tourism Shanghai Fair

The China International Medical Tourism Shanghai Fair focuses on the health industry in the new era and starts from advances in international medicine. It intends to build a platform for academic exchange and cooperation, through promoting development and by making contributions to the global biological medicine and health industry.

Big Data Expo

The Big Data Expo highlights the global vision, national interests, industry roles and corporate responsibilities, serving as a platform for global big data professionals, organizations, and entrepreneurs coming to jointly discuss industry trends while presenting and analyzing their achievements and experience.

Beijing International Tourism Expo

The Beijing International Tourism Expo (BITE) is one of the most influential and famous international exhibition which has been successfully held for 16 years. BITE is an important exchange and trade platform for promoting global tourism resources and products and stimulating tourism consumption.

Highlights

- B2B+B2C effective operating
- Exclusive B2B matchmaking
- Fam-trip, hosted buyer program for international buyers

Smart Factory & Automation Technology Expo

The Smart Factory & Automation Technology Expo explores the areas of machine vision, IoT and big data, industrial software, industrial robots, system integration, smart warehousing and logistics, and other exhibitions involving advanced technologies of smart factories. The exhibition brings innovative achievements and technical solutions for smart manufacturing to consumer electronics, automotive electronics, communications electronics, and other electronic manufacturing companies, especially for automotive electronics, mobile phone casings, 3D glass covers, and touch screens.

4YFN Shanghai

4YFN Shanghai is Asia's largest exhibition for the mobile industry, supporting start-ups, investors and companies to create, discover, and launch new ventures together. The exhibition offers the opportunity to showcase your company, products, or services to a highly relevant international audience.

Sinophex—Pharmaceutical Equipment Exhibition

Sinophex—Pharmaceutical Equipment Exhibition is a professional platform for learning, communication, and cooperation in China's pharmaceutical equipment industry and it intends to provide Chinese pharmaceutical companies with environmental protection, cleanliness, raw materials, preparations, and biochemical equipment.

International Building & Construction Trade Fair

The International Building & Construction Trade Fair specializes in many of the building and construction essentials, such as green building material, chemical building material, building hardware, installation and tools, renovation products, construction glass products and processing technology, wall materials, plaster and gypsum, wallpaper, heat and noise insulating materials, marble, granite, stone slate, artificial stone products, ceramic tiles, brick tiles, mosaic tiles, quarry tiles, pavement tiles, staircase, components, processing equipment, windows, doors, gate, facades, blinds, casement section, sunshade, mosquito net, and accessories including curtains, which are displayed in this show.

Overseas Property & Immigration & Investment Fair

The Shanghai International Property Management Industry Exhibition is an important platform for strengthening cooperation between upstream and downstream enterprises in the property management industry chain and for promoting common development at home and abroad. The scope of the exhibition covers property management companies, smart community O2O, smart parking systems and equipment, smart security, smart home, self-service facilities, property uniforms, environmental greening maintenance, community and commercial entertainment facilities, energy-saving solutions, and other sectors.

China (Shenzhen) International Logistics and Supply Chain Fair

The China (Shenzhen) International Logistics and Supply Chain Fair (CILF) has earned a popular reputation. As an effective and wide exchange platform for all players in logistics, transport, and relevant industries all over the world, the CILF attracts numerous international well-known firms coming to exhibit and further promote the international influence of China's logistics industry.

China International Logistics Equipment & Technology Exhibition

The China International Logistics Equipment & Technology Exhibition is the largest international exhibition in the logistics equipment industry in south China. As a professional logistics exhibition, we always keep the market frontier, upholding technology and innovation. The advanced concept of service, based on the south China market, provides customers with a professional and efficient display platform.

Shenzhen International 3D Printing Industry Exhibition

The Shenzhen International 3D Printing Industry Exhibition is a convergence of well-known brands, 3D printing, and intelligent manufacturing into the wonderful world of new products, new technologies, and new processes, allowing 3D printing and intelligent manufacturing professionals—more than 25,000 professionals—to gather and share the best practices in the industry while discovering the hottest product launches.

China Franchise Expo Shanghai

China Franchise exhibition is supported by the China National Chain Management Association, the only national industry organization in the domestic chain. The scope of exhibiting enterprises includes three major industries such as catering, retail and service, service providers, and industrial organizations. It is an industrywide exhibition.

Author's Statement

China is the greatest economic success story of the last 50 years. It has been the largest exporter of goods since 2009 and the world's largest trading nation in the world since 2013. This position was previously held by the United States. Since the "opening-up" policy was introduced in the late 1970s, China has changed beyond recognition. A Soviet-style planned economy has been transformed into a vibrant and incredibly dynamic, market-oriented system that helped 600 million people to rise from poverty. While many of the world's major economies are still struggling to recover from the economic slowdown, China's economy has grown at just under 10 percent every year for more than 30 years, overtaking Japan in 2010 to become the world's second largest economy. Traditionally, China has provided low-cost manufacturing solutions for the global market. However, due to the sharp decline in exports following the 2008 global downturn, the Chinese manufacturing industry has responded by quickly moving up the value chain.

China is an important export market for many American, British, and European companies, and understanding the requirements is a key element of export success. There are still challenges, but the business environment in China and market access have improved for exporters. China climbed the World Bank ease of doing business ranking by 15 places in 2019. It is now higher than many European countries. Technical regulations, standards, and conformity assessment play a vital role in any company's competitiveness both at home and in the global marketplace. China's distance from your home country, its sheer size, and market complexity make it a unique challenge. On the one hand, the opportunities are too great to ignore. On the other, the risk and price of a failed market entry can be especially high. At the same time, quality Chinese market research is not something that the average business—or even the average market research company—can do. As a result, some companies actually do *less* research than they normally would when launching their products into their home markets and get burned. Don't be one of them!

Trading With China aims to assist Western businesses, entrepreneurs, and international business development executives to export their products, services, and technology to China. It is designed to work as a step-by-step guide to those who want to enter and remain competitive in this tremendously challenging and profitable market that is China. It contains practical advice, suggestions, key models, industry information, updated data, and strategy options for different types of companies.

It details all relevant procedures, categorizes opportunities and challenges by industry sector and geographical region, and discusses in-depth key topics such as the market barriers, distribution channels, import requirements, labeling, and operational challenges. Topics covered in this volume also include relevant rules, regulations, documentation, management issues, and applicable strategies related to the import of various types of goods or services into China, to help you make a more informed decision before starting your export adventure.

Index

OTHER TITLES IN THE INTERNATIONAL BUSINESS COLLECTION

S. Tamer Cavusgil, Manchester Business School,
Michael Czinkota, Georgetown, and
Gary Knight, Willamette University, Editors

- *The Chinese e-Merging Market* by Danai Krokou
- *The Chinese Market* by Danai Krokou
- *Creative Solutions to Global Business Negotiations, Third Edition* by Claude Cellich
- *Exporting* by Laurent Houlier and John Blaskey
- *Global Trade Strategies* by Michel Borgeon and Claude Cellich
- *Doing Business in Germany* by Andra Riemhofer
- *Major Business and Technology Trends Shaping the Contemporary World* by Hamid Yeganeh
- *Entering the Chinese e-Merging Market* by Danai Krokou
- *In Search for the Soul of International Business* by Michael R. Czinkota
- *Doing Business in the United States* by Anatoly Zhuplev, Matthew Stefl, and Andrew Rohm
- *Globalization Alternatives* by Joseph Mark Munoz

Concise and Applied Business Books

The Collection listed above is one of 30 business subject collections that Business Expert Press has grown to make BEP a premiere publisher of print and digital books. Our concise and applied books are for...

- Professionals and Practitioners
- Faculty who adopt our books for courses
- Librarians who know that BEP's Digital Libraries are a unique way to offer students ebooks to download, not restricted with any digital rights management
- Executive Training Course Leaders
- Business Seminar Organizers

Business Expert Press books are for anyone who needs to dig deeper on business ideas, goals, and solutions to everyday problems. Whether one print book, one ebook, or buying a digital library of 110 ebooks, we remain the affordable and smart way to be business smart. For more information, please visit www.businessexpertpress.com, or contact sales@businessexpertpress.com.